Business Process Improvement Toolbox

Also available from ASQ Quality Press

Creativity, Innovation, and Quality
Paul E. Plsek

Quality Problem Solving
Gerald F. Smith

Root Cause Analysis: A Tool for Total Quality Management
Paul F. Wilson, Larry D. Dell, and Gaylord F. Anderson

Mapping Work Processes
Dianne Galloway

Quality Quotes
Hélio Gomes

Let's Work Smarter, Not Harder: How to Engage Your Entire Organization in the Execution of Change
Michael Caravatta

The Change Agents' Handbook: A Survival Guide for Quality Improvement Champions
David W. Hutton

Understanding and Applying Value-Added Assessment: Eliminating Business Process Waste
William E. Trischler

To request a complimentary catalog of ASQ Quality Press publications, call 800-248-1946.

Business Process Improvement Toolbox

Bjørn Andersen

ASQ Quality Press

Milwaukee, Wisconsin

Business Process Improvement Toolbox
Bjørn Andersen

Library of Congress Cataloging-in-Publication Data

Andersen, Bjørn.
    Business improvement toolbox / Bjørn Andersen.
        p.   cm.
    Includes bibliographic referencews and index
    ISBN 0-87389-438-3
        1. Reengineering (Management)   2. Benchmarking
    (Management)   3. Reengineering (Management)—Charts, diagrams,
    etc.   I. Title.
    HD58.87.A53   1998
    658.4'063—dc21   98-14191
                                                               CIP

10 9 8 7 6 5 4 3 2

ISBN: 0-87389-438-3

Acquisitions Editor: Ken Zielske
Project Editor: Annemieke Koudstaal
Production Coordinator: Shawn Dohogne

ASQ Mission: The American Society for Quality advances individual and organizational performance excellence worldwide by providing opportunities for learning, quality improvement, and knowledge exchange.

Attention: Bookstores, Wholesalers, Schools and Corporations:
ASQ Quality Press books, videotapes, audiotapes, and software are available at quantity discounts with bulk purchases for business, educational, or instructional use. For information, please contact ASQ Quality Press at 800-248-1946, or write to ASQ Quality Press, P.O. Box 3005, Milwaukee, WI 53201-3005.

To place orders or to request a free copy of the ASQ Quality Press Publications Catalog, including ASQ membership information, call 800-248-1946. Visit our web site at http://www.asq.org.
Printed in the United States of America

∞ Printed on acid-free paper

American Society for Quality

Quality Press
611 East Wisconsin Avenue
Milwaukee, Wisconsin 53202
Call toll free 800-248-1946
http://www.asq.org
http://standardsgroup.asq.org

Advance Praise for *Business Process Improvement Toolbox*

Dr. Andersen has thoughtfully prepared a very fine reference to a full range of useful improvement tools. This book places the improvement approaches in context and offers a plan for their effective use. I recommend the book as a highly worthwhile addition to any process improvement library.

> Dr. Robert C. Camp
> Principal of the Best Practices Institute™

I find *Business Process Improvement Toolbox* a masterful integration of traditional quality tools . . . . For an enterprise truly concerned with developing seamless relationships internally and externally to itself, the book provides a pragmatic view of process definition, improvement planning, suggested tools for achieving the plans, and methods for measuring the extent to which processes have been improved. The reader is led carefully through the concepts, the methods, and the abundance of useful examples. Even templates are included! I'm truly impressed with the fresh and simple approach to the use of business process improvement tools.

> Dr. John D. Hromi
> Professor Emeritus, Rochester Institute of Technology and former President of ASQ

The *Business Process Improvement Toolbox* by Bjørn Andersen, in my view contains more tools than any other similar book and should prove to be a best seller among quality and improvement professionals alike, around the world. In my very first reading, I felt like I was in a Quality Hardware Store, every tool I wanted to refer to, was there. Congratulations, Bjørn for this fine work.

> Turk Enustun
> Senior Quality Consultant and Director, Corporate Benchmarking, Eastman Kodak Company

Business Process Improvement Toolbox presents a comprehensive set of improvement tools in a logical manner and indicates their use in a company-wide improvement process. This approach is an advantage compared to many other similar books and makes it very useful for practitioners in companies striving for improvement.

> Asbjørn Aune
> Professor, Norwegian University of Science and Technology and member of the International
> Academy of Quality

Contents

Figures

Tables

Preface

Like many others who work with Total Quality Management, improvement, performance measurement, and so forth, I have written books on isolated tools—in my case, benchmarking. At times, the interest in this one tool has probably clouded the ability to view improvement work as a more coherent whole. My position is that this also applies to many of my colleagues. There are countless good books about different philosophies, tools, and techniques for improvement, but very few show how these fit together into a larger whole. This argument, however, does not lead to a claim that this book does.

But unlike many of the volumes that focus on isolated tools and methods, the objective of this book is to illustrate how they can be used together in a coherent process-improvement system. Most people agree that business processes are today's view of an organization, and that these processes need to be improved. To that end, this book sets forth to show how process documentation, performance measurement, and improvement tools can be combined into a complete toolbox. How to use these many tools is described in the framework of an overall improvement model, including the phases of improvement planning, improvement, performance measurement, and performance evaluation. This gives a solid foundation for a continuous journey of process improvement. Within each of these phases, the improvement-oriented organization will find tools that serve different purposes.

In line with the pattern of the last book I co-wrote, *The Benchmarking Handbook: Step-by-Step Instructions*, this is also a very practical book. Rather than focusing on basic theory or academic deductions, I focus on describing an improvement process that can be used in real life. All available tools are presented with clear descriptions of the procedures for using them, as well as their applications. For every tool, there is also an example of its use. Because this is a practical handbook in the area of process improvement, I have included ready-to-use templates for most of the tools that can be copied and used directly. The book is organized according to an overall improvement process and includes, in order, process documentation, performance measurement, improvement planning, the toolbox for improvement, and, finally, a large case study.

Scholarly inspiration to write this book has come from a long list of sources. Through tight cooperation with Harald and Reinholdt Bredrup and Karianne Prytz in the TOPP program, many elements in this jigsaw puzzle were developed. Others fell into place through participation in a number of benchmarking studies, not in the least together with Per-Gaute Pettersen in the TOPP Benchmarking project. In addition, the entire faculty of the Department of Production and Quality Engineering at the Norwegian University of Science and Technology—as well as SINTEF Industrial Management, Production Engineering—has helped form my academic position.

Finally, my wife, Hilde M. Andersen, has been an important support through discussions of the structure of the book—contents, presentation format, and so forth. It is amazing how much clarifying input a person can give who has her education in other fields. The number of typing errors would also have been higher without her help in proofreading.

Finally, I would like to express my hopes for this book: that you, the reader, will look through it, hopefully find the thoughts and processes interesting, and use it actively as a dictionary in your improvement process.

Bjørn Andersen

CHAPTER 1

Does a Company Consist of Departments or Processes?

Both, of course. But viewing it as consisting of processes offers advantages, and such an approach is also historically correct. This book deals with how to conduct improvement, and is based on improvement efforts directed at business processes. This chapter briefly explains what is meant by the term *business processes*.

1.1 From Processes to Departments to Business Processes

At some point in history, man began coordinating his actions to be able to perform more extensive or complex tasks than what could be accomplished alone. We must assume that such coordination, the first type of what might be termed *enterprises*, was initiated by a demand. For example, when a farmer hired helpers for different tasks like plowing, sowing, and reaping, the background was that the work was too extensive for the farmer to manage on his own. Focus was on satisfying a demand for food by performing the processes necessary. In other words, the actions were process-oriented. The work force was not split into ploughers, sowers, and reapers; rather the hired help carried out the tasks necessary.

Soon the extent and complexity of the tasks expanded further, and the number of people in different coordinated enterprises increased. For as long as enterprises with more than a few employees have been in existence, they have probably been organized into departments. It was no longer feasible to maintain a workforce where everybody performed each single task. The tasks became so complex that the individual worker had to specialize. Therefore, a logical step was to form departments consisting of individuals with similar areas of expertise. This expanded into a tradition with a solid foothold in all types of organizations—commercial, public, and ideal. Until a few years ago, this way of organizing was highly dominant and had completely replaced the original way of aligning the organization more directly according to the work to be performed. Organizing people and work into departments certainly provided, and still provides, some benefits:

- People were allowed to specialize within their field of expertise, thus developing a highly refined set of skills.

- Costs from centralizing various functions (for example, finance, personnel, maintenance) were lowered.

- The workplace was made more secure; everyone knew where they belonged and which tasks they were supposed to perform.

- The organizational structure was more clearly defined and could easily be drawn and presented.

Thus, we can safely claim that modern enterprises consist of functional departments, while at the same time performing processes. Figure 1.1 depicts a typical enterprise with its vertical departments and horizontal processes that run through these (Andersen and Pettersen, 1996). It has lately become obvious that this contradiction between mode or organization and tasks has created several problems.

As soon as people have been established within a square in an organization chart with departments as those shown in Figure 1.1, it often seems as if the lines of this square become solid boundaries within which they must remain. Communication across the borders is limited, and members of a department will perform only those tasks that naturally belong to the area of responsibility of their department. Each department seeks to maximize its influence and authority while at the same time optimize the department's performance level. The result is usually that the whole is far from being more than the sum of the individual elements, and in the worst case, far less. Each department suboptimizes within its area of responsibility, which in turn leads to conflicting objectives and conflicting actions between different departments. The total performance level of the organization is naturally in line with this (Rolstadås, 1995).

A company that manufactures elements for the building industry delivers regular stock goods, standard goods that are not stored, and special variants. One of the company's main problems has been that the demand for production capacity has been very unstable—sometimes far above the capacity limit, and

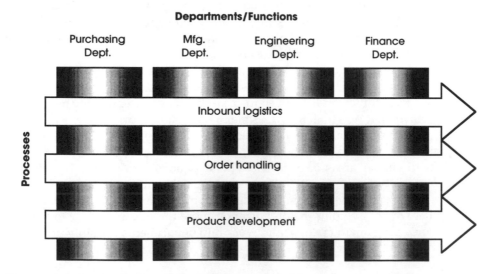

Figure 1.1.   The contradiction between vertical departments and horizontal processes.

at other times with much free capacity. In periods of high demand, delivery times have increased dramatically, which has turned out to be a problem in the market. In the company's monitoring of the sales department, a central performance measure was fulfillment of the sales quota for each period. This led to a situation in which a salesperson, when the quota for a period had been completed, put all later orders "in the drawer" for the next period. This way, the employee made sure he had a reserve before the next period started that could help fill his quota if sales should be slow. This, of course, contributed to the uneven demand for production capacity and the sometimes-prolonged delivery times. At the same time, important information was being withheld from the planning department that, in turn, could have given better production plans. The salesperson's optimization of his/her own performance level, as it was being measured by the company, led to an overall performance level for the company that was far from the best achievable.

These problems, and others, have formed the basis for the last year's changes—from viewing the company as a number of departments to focusing on the business processes being performed. Several issues make this a logical transition:

- Every process has a customer, and focusing on the process ensures better focus on the customer.

- The value creation with regard to the end product takes place in horizontal processes.

- By defining process boundaries and the customers and suppliers of the processes, better communication and well-understood requirements can be achieved.

- By managing entire processes that run through many departments rather than managing individual departments, the risk of suboptimization is reduced.

- By appointing so-called *process owners*, who are responsible for the process, the traditional fragmentation of responsibility often seen in a functional organization is avoided.

- Managing processes provides a better foundation for controlling time and resources.

Many of these elements are based on the fact that every single process has both a supplier and a customer, as shown in Figure 1.2. This so-called *customer/supplier model* is central in the thinking underlying the process view.

What, then, is a business process?

1.2   Definition of a Business Process

Business process: business and process. First, a look at the element *process*. One basic definition of a process is:

> "... *a logic series of related transactions that converts input to results or output.*"

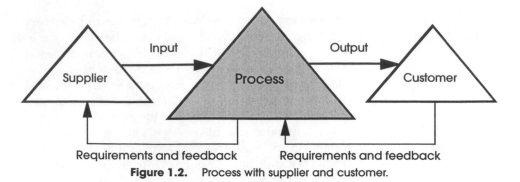

Figure 1.2.   Process with supplier and customer.

To separate a company's processes from any other form of processes, the word *business* has been added to form the term *business process*. A business process can be defined in a number of different ways, but this book is based on the following definition (Ericsson, 1993):

- A chain of logical connected, repetitive activities that
- utilizes the enterprise's resources to
- refine an object (physical or mental)
- for the purpose of achieving specified and measurable results/products for
- internal or external customers.

A main point is that any business process has a customer, either external or internal. Based on this definition, almost all activities within a company can be seen as a business process or part of a business process. What are the most central business processes, then?

1.3   Classification of Business Processes

There are a number of ways to classify business. Many leading companies with respect to process orientation have conducted thorough analyses of their own enterprises and have compiled lists of their central processes. For example, both Xerox and IBM have made lists of a different number of processes. These lists are thus specially designed for the tasks carried out in these companies.

At the same time, different interest organizations have done a similar job, but on a more general basis. The purpose for these organizations has been to create lists so general that they are relevant for a high number of companies. Two contributors in this group are the International Benchmarking Clearinghouse (IBC) in Houston and the European Foundation for Quality Management (EFQM).

Modeling enterprises, and as a part of this, defining general sets of business processes, has come to be a field of its own, occupying many academics. For example, researchers at the University of Plymouth have defined a hierarchy of business processes that spans five levels and is very extensive. The processes are divided into the three main groups: "operate," "manage," and "support."

A somewhat simpler and more practically oriented approach can be found in the work performed in the Norwegian TOPP program, a research program on productivity managed from NTNU/SINTEF in Trondheim. To create a foundation for developing methods for self assessment and benchmarking, a framework of business processes was developed. In line with the thinking of Porter's value chain, the processes were divided into primary and support processes. In addition, some of the support processes were further separated into a new class termed *development processes*. The three groups were defined as follows:

- *Primary processes* are the central and value-creating processes of the enterprise. They run straight through the company, from activities on the customer side to receiving supplies from vendors.

- *Support processes* are not directly value-creating processes, but rather activities needed to support the primary processes. This includes activities like financial and personnel management.

- *Development processes* are processes that are supposed to bring the value chain with its primary and support processes to a higher level of performance. Examples are product development and supplier development.

The results from the TOPP program were further developed in the ENAPS project (European Network for Advanced Performance Studies), a European Commission-funded project aiming at developing a European benchmarking database. A slightly different approach was adopted in terms of naming the classes, but the three main groups from TOPP were maintained. However, in ENAPS, the primary processes were named *business processes* and split into four main processes, each with sub-processes below these. The two remaining groups were called *secondary processes*, split into support and evolution processes Figure 1.3 shows the ENAPS framework and the individual processes included in it (ENAPS, 1997).

The purpose of this section is not to give a detailed presentation of this framework but rather aims to give an impression of what are considered the central business

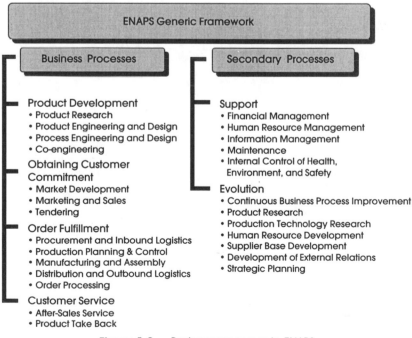

Figure 1.3.   Business processes in ENAPS.

processes. This will later contribute to forming a foundation for different activities aimed at improving the business processes of the enterprise.

REFERENCES

Andersen, Bjørn, and Per-Gaute Pettersen. *The Benchmarking Handbook: Step-by-Step Instructions*. Chapman & Hall, London, England, 1996.

ENAPS. *Deliverable F3-4: A Set of Refined and Agreed Performance Indicators Defined by Business Processes*. ENAPS, Galway, Ireland, 1997.

Ericsson Quality Institute. *Business Process Management*. Ericsson, Gothenburg, Sweden, 1993.

Hammer, M., and J. Champy. *Re-engineering the Corporation: A Manifesto for Business Revolution*. Harper Business, New York, New York, USA, 1993.

Rolstadås, Asbjørn, ed. *Performance Management: A Business Process Benchmarking Approach*. Chapman & Hall, London, England, 1995.

CHAPTER 2

Conducting and Organizing Improvements

As the preceding chapter offered a basic introduction to business processes, this chapter briefly discusses improvement in general, and presents an overall improvement process and how improvements should be organized in an enterprise.

2.1   Why is Improvement Necessary?

Many issues, both internal and external, have caused improvements to become necessary in today's marketplace:

- The performance level of most processes shows a tendency to decrease over time unless forces are exerted to maintain it. This means that to simply maintain the current standards, it is necessary to perform some degree of maintenance. If additionally we want to create improvement and renewal, this requires efforts beyond pure maintenance, as shown in Figure 2.1.

- If an organization does not improve, you can be quite certain the competitors will. Should the unlikely scenario occur that neither an organization nor the competitors improve, there are always other actors willing to enter the market segment.

- Today's customers are becoming more and more demanding and, frankly, are spoiled. Supply and the quality of the supply are ever increasing, which in turn cause the expectations to rise dramatically. If it is not always possible to *exceed* the expectations, which is the ideal situation, they at least have to be *met*. If not, you are guaranteed to lose the customer.

Generally, this means that what was maybe quite satisfactory a few years ago, today barely passes, and quite certainly will soon be below expectations. It is therefore irrelevant to discuss whether we *have* to improve; the question is rather *how much* and *how fast* the improvement should be.

There is, of course, no definitive answer to this, but a rather general one is that continuous improvement combined with breakthroughs is needed. In this respect, it

7

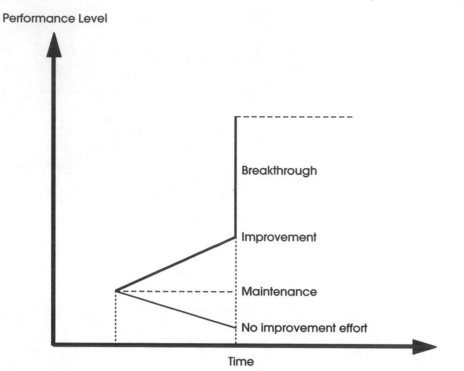

Figure 2.1.   Without maintenance and improvement, the performance level decreases.

is worth pointing out that experience indicates that an organization that emphasizes continuous improvement usually also possesses the creativity and attitude toward improvement necessary to create an occasional breakthrough. If trying exclusively to achieve a breakthrough and neglecting the continuous improvement activity, it might prove difficult to create a breakthrough when needed. It is also a fact that the different improvement tools available are more or less suitable for different improvement rates and scope. This will be further discussed in chapters 6 and 13. Regardless of which tool is being used, business processes are a good starting point for the improvement work. How to create this starting point through documenting the organization's business processes is the main theme of chapter 3.

2.2   A Model for Performance Improvement

The last subject to be treated in this chapter is an overall model for improvement work within an organization. The model was developed in the previously mentioned TOPP program and is depicted in Figure 2.2 (Bredrup, 1995).

The upper part of the model represents a cycle of activities performed in the improvement process and consists of planning, improvement, review, and action. It is difficult to define where the cycle starts, simply because it is a cycle. Depending on the enterprise using the process and its starting point, we can really start with any one of the three first phases. In this book, however, starting with a performance measurement that helps create a picture of the current situation is recommended, preferably through the use of so-called *self assessment*. (This method will be treated in more detail in chapter 5.) The lower part of the model indicates which types of input can

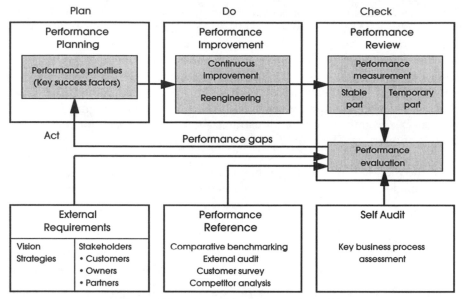

Figure 2.2. Overall improvement model.

be used during the performance evaluation. The activities of the improvement processes are described as follows.

First phase, the performance evaluation, is as the name implies an evaluation of the performance level. When performing the improvement process for the first time, this will constitute an introductory measurement of the current status that will form the basis for the planning of improvements. At later cycles of the process, this will represent an evaluation of the performance level after improvements have been implemented. When this process starts rolling, each time this phase is performed, the measurements can be compared with the results from the preceding run, thus indicating whether sufficient improvement was achieved and if the effort had any effect. At the same time, the company's performance level can be compared to different external reference points that can provide further impulses for the next round of performance planning. (This comparison with external references is often termed *benchmarking* and is covered in chapter 10.)

During the performance planning, priorities are set with regard to which areas or processes that should be improved. This prioritization is conducted based on the performance evaluation, the organization's strategy, and the definition of its critical success factors. The main result from this phase will be a prioritized list defining the areas that should be improved. Another important element of this phase is that organizational responsibility for planning and performing improvements is appointed. Instead of starting activities based on individual initiatives, this process must be consciously managed to ensure that activities truly are started and are in accordance with each other and the company's priorities. (Improvement planning is treated in chapter 5.)

Performance improvement is the active part of this process. In this phase, improvements are implemented in line with the priorities defined in the preceding phase. The model does not indicate how improvement can be achieved, but it is assumed that both smaller, continuous improvements and more extensive breakthroughs will be a part of the complete results. Specific tools for use in this phase are described in more detail later in the book.

Once this cyclical process of constantly occurring improvements has been set into motion, the effects of the improvement initiatives will be measured in the performance evaluation phase. If they seem to have produced satisfactory results during the action phase, the improved processes will be defined as the new standard.

Those familiar with the work of W. Edwards Deming will see that this improvement model is based on the principles of the Deming wheel (Deming, 1986). The Deming wheel, or the cycle of plan, do, check, and act, is shown in Figure 2.3.

It describes a control loop that illustrates a general approach for conducting continuous improvement. The activities of the four phases are:

- In the planning phase, the problem is analyzed and activities to remedy it are planned—that is, improvement planning.

- In the do phase, the activities planned in the previous phase are carried out. The purpose is primarily to experiment with the solution.

- In the evaluation, or check, phase, measurements are made to evaluate whether the activities had any effect on the problem—that is, a performance evaluation.

- Finally, in the action phase, the process is modified according to the activities that were confirmed to give results. After having performed the four phases, the result is an improved process.

The main purpose of the Deming wheel, besides describing a systematic approach to improvement, is that the wheel should be set into motion through continuously performing this process.

2.3 Organizing Improvements

With reference to the overall improvement process of Figure 2.2, it is possible to outline some coarse guidelines for the organization of improvement activities. Top management must be responsible for the higher-level evaluation of the organization's performance level. If this is done through self assessment, it is the responsibility of

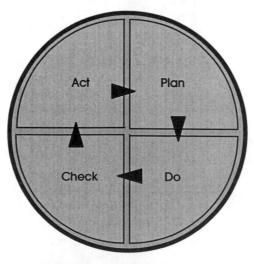

Figure 2.3. The Deming wheel.

top management to maintain the assessment tool and to initiate measurement. Furthermore, it is also top management's obvious responsibility to prioritize what improvement actions should be launched. This is especially true for larger and more resource-demanding projects but does not imply that smaller, local initiatives cannot be started without specific pressure from the top. When it comes to both performance evaluation and planning, it is important that the responsibility is placed with one single person, even if it is the collective responsibility of top management to perform these tasks. If these extremely important tasks are left to be performed whenever someone accidentally remembers, it is very likely that they will be given a low priority.

Specific improvement projects can be carried out with great advantage by teams or groups formed to deal with each project. These are different from more permanent groups whose tasks are to continuously work with improvement initiatives. (Different types of such groups are described in chapter 11.)

Both categories of teams—temporary and permanent—are usually formed on the initiative from management, and the responsibility for establishing teams to take care of prioritized improvement projects must reside with top management. When forming a project team, there are some guidelines that should be kept in mind. First of all, the team should fill the following roles:

- Team leader—that is, a person who has the overall responsibility for calling meetings, monitoring the progress of the project, making sure minutes are prepared and that necessary information is gathered and distributed, and so on. Many of these tasks can usually be delegated, but the responsibility remains with the team leader. It is quite common, but not necessary, that this role is given to the person on the team with the highest position in the organizational hierarchy.

- Link to or support from management, either through representation on the team from management or by giving someone authority to represent management.

- Process owner or the person who in other ways is responsible for the whole or most of the process to be focused on.

- Other persons involved in the process, preferably from a cross-section of the organizational units the process runs through. It is extremely important to make sure that the team does not consist of people who really are located above or on the side of the process to be improved. If those who will later have to change their routines are not involved in the team, making the necessary changes might be hard to do.

- A customer of the process, internal or external. Along with a process view comes a commitment to viewing the customer of the process as the most important part of the puzzle. By involving the customer on the team, it is possible to make sure that the customer's views are adhered to in the improvement activity.

- A supplier to the process, internal or external. In the same way that any process has a customer, any process also has a supplier that provides some input. The supplier is to a smaller or larger extent a part of the factors that shape the performance level of the process through the input being supplied, and should therefore be included in the improvement activity.

- Possibly some kind of external assistance in cases where the improvement tool to be used is new to the team.

One person can, by the way, take on several roles. From experience, such a team should not have more than six or seven members, even though this obviously is dependent on the scope and complexity of the project. At the same time, care should be taken not to establish a team that is too small, as this might hamper the team's ability to perform its tasks and undermine a broader sense of ownership of the project's results.

When selecting the members of such a team, the following requirements for candidates should be posed:

- Time to participate actively and whole-heartedly in the work. Instead of including key personnel that never have the time to participate, choose persons that can make an effort in the project. On the other hand, there are usually some people you cannot do without, and these will have to set aside the necessary time.

- Competencies and knowledge—knowledge about both the organization and the relevant business processes, and competencies in the tool that is expected to be used. Alternatively, training in use of the tool must be provided at the outset of the project.

- Motivation—that is, a desire to work on improving the selected process. A person selected against his or her will is an unsuitable member of an improvement team.

- The ability to cooperate, listen, and communicate, as this is a typical team effort that is less suited for the traditional silent loner.

- Credibility and respect in the organization, to ensure impact when presenting results from the project and proceeding with effective implementation of improvements.

Finally, a warning must be issued against recruiting members based on the thinking, "You have nothing better to do; go participate in this improvement project!"

A manufacturing company with approximately 400 employees started an improvement project connected to the procurement process and its link to the more general logistics processes. It was decided to establish an improvement team that would work on the project. The team included the procurement manager, the logistics manager, and the manager for production planning. In addition, external assistance was hired to be part of the team.

This composition had several negative consequences:

- These three persons traveled quite extensively and were generally rather busy, which made it difficult to arrange meetings or have any work done between meetings.

- The fact that they were located quite high up in the organizational hierarchy meant that they were less involved in the operative performing of processes. Thus, the knowledge about the processes within the team was too low to enable any detailed documentation of the process or generation of improvement suggestions.

- Each of the members of the team had a large degree of responsibility within his own area and felt personally responsible for the performance level within it. It was therefore difficult to admit weaknesses and problems, and very few constructive improvement suggestions achieved broad support from the team.

It probably would have been wise to allow more operative personnel into the team.

Figure 2.4. The organization of the main content of the book.

The main content of this book is presented according to the sequence of the most central activities of the improvement work. The first two tasks are to document the organization's business processes and to create a system for measuring and evaluating the performance level of these processes. These two activities really fall outside the overall improvement process, as they constitute basic conditions that must be in place before such a cyclical process can be started. Thereafter follow in sequence self assessment with performance evaluation, improvement planning, and finally the improvement activities themselves. The next chapters will follow the outline as shown in Figure 2.4.

REFERENCES

Bredrup, Harald. "Performance Measurement in a Changing Competitive Industrial Environment: Breaking the Financial Paradigm." Ph.D. thesis, Norwegian Institute of Technology, Trondheim, Norway, 1995.

Deming, W. Edwards. *Out of the Crisis: Quality, Productivity and Competitive Position.* Cambridge University Press, Cambridge, Massachusetts, USA, 1986.

CHAPTER 3

Process Documentation

A general rule if wanting to improve something is that it is necessary to know in advance how the current state of things are. This is highly true for business processes as well. If you do not know how the process looks and works today, it will be very difficult to know which improvement initiatives can be started and whether they will work at all. Documenting one's own process should therefore always be the first step in any improvement activity.

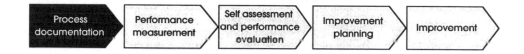

3.1 Should the Business Processes Be Documented One by One or All at Once?

Documenting business processes can principally take place at two different points in time:

- One by one in connection with projects involving the specific process; or

- All at once at the start of the general "improvement journey."

On one hand, you might select an approach where a process is not documented until a project or some other activity is started to improve it. Process documentation will in such cases be the first activity of the project and serve several purposes:

- A common understanding within the improvement team of the content of the process is created: its activities, results, and who performs the different steps of it.

- The scope of the process is defined, as are boundaries to adjacent processes.

- It is possible to define more specific problems within the main process, if desired.

This approach works quite well in practice. There is no need to document many processes at the start, as this is rather carried out when the need arises. For smaller organizations lacking resources or for organizations where the business processes change rapidly, this is probably the preferred approach.

The other way is to initiate the "improvement journey" is by going through the entire organization and documenting all or most of the business processes. As mentioned in chapter 1, this might involve everything from 15 to 100 business processes. It is obviously not possible to cover every single process being performed within the enterprise; the purpose is to document the most important ones. The advantages of this approach are:

- By involving many employees in this work, a positive attitude and improvement motivation are often created that are useful in later projects.

- After having undertaken such an exercise, top management will have formed a very good overview of the organization and the need for specific improvement projects. In this respect, this task helps form a foundation for the necessary prioritization of improvement areas described in the improvement process (see Figure 2.2).

- The insight into the individual processes that is created during the documentation work often makes it possible to pinpoint elements of individual processes that can be improved.

To the extent that the time and resources necessary for such an introductory process documentation can be mustered, this is probably the most valuable approach. To follow the scheme for improvement described in this book, this approach is also the one that is recommended. Through such a start of the improvement activities, the necessary groundwork is laid for conducting a self assessment that the ensuing improvement initiatives will be based on.

When comparing these two approaches, consider that many companies already possess a good framework for an overall process documentation in the shape of procedures developed for ISO-9000 certification. In this material, there are usually both process descriptions and some type of graphical representation. This material is highly suitable for building on, thus reducing the workload.

However, bear in mind that the procedures and processes of the quality handbook often reflect the *ideal* situation, not always the *real*. In the improvement work, it is important to start out from the real situation, to be able to identify problem areas. Furthermore, it is a fact that most processes are to some extent changing, often rendering these descriptions inaccurate or directly erroneous. Much extra work can be saved by checking the quality of this material before using it. The objective must always be to document the process as *it is really performed* today, not the way it was *supposed* to be performed.

3.2   Identifying the Business Processes

Before documenting one or more business processes, be sure that the business processes of the enterprise have been identified. This can at times be rather difficult, as it rarely is obvious which processes are undertaken by the different departments in a functionally organized company. Two complementary routes to such an understanding can be utilized (Peppard, 1998). The most direct way is to simply generate a list of the business processes believed to be encompassed by the organization. Such a job will often be based on existing process descriptions or procedures written for ISO-9000 certification or similar purposes.

A more rewarding and systematic route is to map out the following sequence of elements:

- The strategy of the organization, which defines and is shaped by:

- Stakeholders (that is, organizations, institutions, or persons affected by or with a vested interest in the organization and its business processes) who hold:

- Expectations with regard to products or services delivered by the organization through:

- The business processes that produce these products or services, and support and enable the production of them.

By going through this set of elements and identifying them in sequence, it is much easier to point to the business processes carried out by the organization and that are necessary in fulfilling the expectations of its stakeholders.

All organizations are able to articulate their strategy, and if not, they are certainly not ready to make the step into process orientation. Once the strategy has been articulated, the identification of stakeholders is relatively easy, even though these include more than the obvious ones (that is, customers). Important stakeholders are also owners, employees, suppliers, governments, local community, and so on, and they all have certain expectations toward the organization. Determining these expectations is again usually fairly straightforward, even if it sometimes involves interaction with the stakeholders.

When all of these expectations have been identified, and preferably ranked according to importance, the identification of the business processes necessary to fulfill them can begin. By nesting backward from the output to the stakeholders through to primary and support processes and input into these, several strings of business processes emerge. Even if this approach does not cover every conceivable process ever performed by the organization, this is actually just as well. Processes not encountered when backtracking from the stakeholders' expectations are hardly crucial in providing satisfaction to them. Thus, if omitted, they will rarely be missed.

When the key business processes have been determined, the real work of documenting each single process can begin. To document a process, the following two-step approach can be useful:

1. Define and describe the process qualitatively, preferably by using the analysis called *relationship mapping*. This includes answering questions like:

    - Who are the customers of the process and what is the output from it?

    - Who are the suppliers to the process and what is the input to it?

    - What are the requirements for the input and output of the process?

    - What is the internal flow of activities of the process?

2. Construct a flowchart.

The remainder of this chapter is devoted to the following techniques for process documentation:

- Relationship mapping
- Flowchart
- Cross-functional flowchart
- Several-leveled flowchart

3.3   Relationship Mapping

Before we can start drawing a detailed flow chart of a process, it is often necessary to create a more overall picture of who are part of the process and what relations they have to one another and to the rest of the world. This is especially true for more extensive and more complicated processes involving a number of individuals or departments. Is the objective, for instance, to document the process of order receipt and delivery of goods to the customer? If so, it can be quite a challenge to put in place the separate steps of the process just like that. In such a situation, relationship mapping is a suitable approach as a first step on the way.

In contrast to an ordinary flow chart, a relationship map does not consider activities or the sequence of such. The map is constructed by placing on a blank sheet the different units, department, or individuals expected to participate in or impact the process. For the process of order receipt and delivery, logical participants would be the sales, planning, production, and procurement departments internally, as well as customers and suppliers. Furthermore, we might imagine that the finance department and external transport companies should be included. A general rule is that it is better to include too many elements, as irrelevant ones will be naturally eliminated throughout the process. It is also possible to draw such a map on several levels, so that each department can be further detailed on a lower level without blurring the overall picture.

After establishing the potential participants in the process, each relationship among them is analyzed to define the type of relationship. Different types of arrows are suitable for this purpose. Elements that in the end remain without any relationships to other elements are removed from the map. In the end, the map is redrawn and will give a good overview about relationships between participants and stakeholders in the process.

Figure 3.1 shows an example of a relationship map for the sample process. The types of arrows used in this map are, of course, only suggestions; there are no standards in this area. It should also be pointed out that the task of conducting such a relationship mapping and the proceeding activities of constructing a flow chart and other tasks related to process documentation must be carried out in a group including the most central participants in the process. The objective is to improve and adjust the process documentation until mutual agreement is reached that it actually reflects how the process is being performed today. On the other hand, you should be careful not to spend too much time creating a very detailed and 100 percent correct depiction of the process. It might very well be that reasonably good documentation achieved quite easily is better than one that is extremely resource-demanding to generate, but is perfect. This must be seen in the context of the later use of the process documentation.

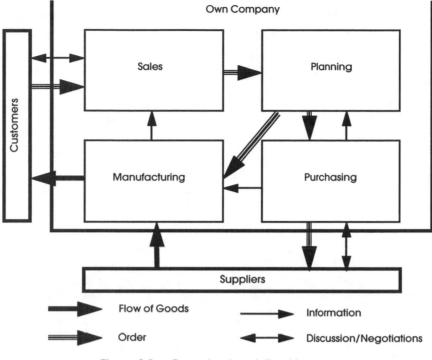

Figure 3.1.   Example of a relationship map.

A large international corporation was organized with one central manufacturing site covering entire Europe and with local dealerships with their own
finished goods inventories in a number of countries. There were clear indications that the supply process, including communicating needs from the
local dealers and distribution to these, was not working satisfactorily. The
company therefore started a project to improve the material flow, starting
with the main manufacturing site. It did, however, prove difficult to form
an overall impression of the flow of information and goods, and it was thus
decided to start the project by drawing a relationship map.

The first step was to collect information from all involved parties about
the most important transactions they were involved in:

- The local dealers based their demand prognoses on twice-yearly sales
  consultations to their main customers.

- Based on aggregated information from these consultations, they
  transmitted their expected demand for the different product families
  to the manufacturing unit.

- Here, the information from all the dealers was further aggregated to
  coarse prognoses for the next six months.

- These formed the basis for negotiations with suppliers about frame
  agreements for the following period.

- Detailed orders were issued by the local dealers every month with a fixed delivery time from the manufacturing site of three weeks.

- The ordered products were either taken from a small finished goods inventory or manufactured before they were sent by car to the dealers.

The local dealers were invoiced only when the goods had been sold to end customers. This produced the relationship map shown in Figure 3.2.

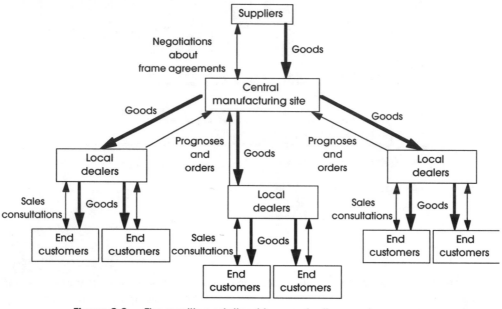

Figure 3.2.   The resulting relationship map for the supply process.

3.4   Flowchart

Very generally, we can say that a flowchart is a graphic depiction of the flow of activities in a process. The use of flowcharts is really a reinforcement of the fact that it is much easier to understand something presented graphically instead of described by words. Put differently, "An image is worth a thousand words."

As the following pages will demonstrate, there are many ways of drawing a flowchart (Andersen and Pettersen, 1996). The most basic way is simply using different symbols to represent activities, and arrows to illustrate the connections between the activities. When it comes to the symbols used, there are a number of variants, including everything from complex pictures to simple boxes and lines. Again, it is not possible to claim that one way is better than another; the point is simply that the users must have a common understanding of the symbols. Some commonly used symbols are:

Start or finishing point

Step or activity in the process

Decision point

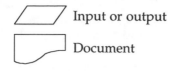

Input or output

Document

In addition, it is possible to indicate on the side of the symbols in the flowchart what resources or equipment are being used and under which conditions the activity is being performed. Returning to the sample process for which a relationship map was constructed, a flowchart might look like the one shown in Figure 3.3.

This chart could obviously have been made more detailed—for instance, by including the suppliers in the process, the negotiations with these and customers, and so on. However, it illustrates the principles for drawing a flowchart. It can, quite justifiably so, be argued that from the chart, it is difficult to see who performs which tasks. This is possible in so-called *cross-functional flowcharts*, which is the next topic.

A group of secretaries in a public office experienced large problems with documents and other materials that, once they were filed, were difficult to find again when they were needed. Among the employees, there was a hunch that some persons used different principles for filing than others. It

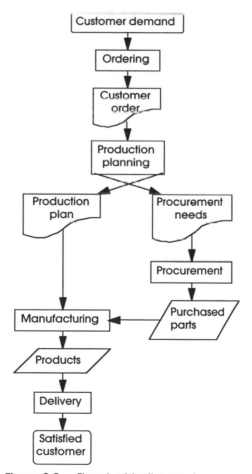

Figure 3.3.   Flowchart for the supply process.

was therefore decided that in a joint effort, how the process was carried out today—and how it *really* should be carried out—should be defined exactly. For this purpose, they wanted to use a flowchart.

The secretaries gathered in a meeting room, armed with a white board and pads of small yellow stickers. It soon became evident that they all performed approximately the same steps when filing documents, but that the criteria for where material was filed varied quite extensively among them. After a heated debate, they were able to agree on both the process and filing criteria. The flowchart in Figure 3.4 was the result of the exercise.

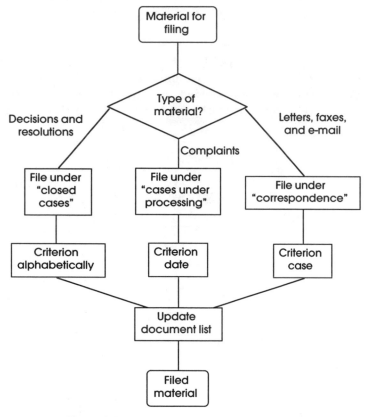

Figure 3.4.   Flowchart for the filing process.

3.5   Cross-functional Flowchart

As has been mentioned, an ordinary flowchart mainly describes what activities are performed in a process. A cross-functional flowchart gives the additional opportunity for indicating who performs the activities, and which functional department they belong to—from which the name arises (Andersen and Pettersen, 1996). Figure 3.5 shows an example, where the ordinary flowchart in Figure 3.3 has been supplemented with more detailed information.

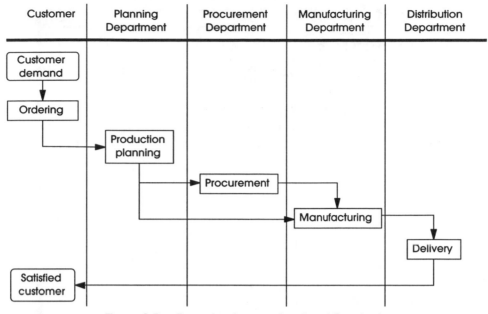

Figure 3.5.   Example of a cross-functional flowchart.

Adding these pieces of information does not take much time compared to the job of describing the sequence of activities itself, but it contributes to a much clearer representation of the process. It is therefore generally recommended to use a cross-functional flowchart. If this is found easier, this can, as was the case in the example, be constructed by first making an ordinary flowchart.

It is also possible in a cross-functional flowchart to display further information. Along the vertical axis, or the horizontal if the process is drawn on a landscape format, information like the following can be added to the chart:

- Time spent so far in the process

- Incurred costs thus far in the process

- Value added

- Degree of completion

This way, the flowchart is able to convey much more information than only the pure sequence of activities in the process. What, then, about the lucidity? Adding more and more information combined with a possibly complex process, the flowchart can at times be difficult to comprehend, at least at a short glance. The answer might be a several-leveled flowchart.

A large company had during the last few years noticed that it was quite expensive to generate the necessary information for financial reporting to various public institutions, including tax authorities. To gain an overview of who did what in the process and where costs were incurred, a cross-functional flowchart was constructed. The resulting chart, shown in Figure 3.6, was well suited for this purpose, and helped reduce costs considerably through a redistribution of responsibilities for different tasks. Not in the

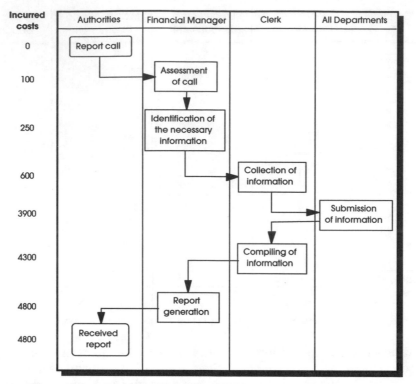

Figure 3.6.   Cross-functional flowchart for the reporting process.

least were efforts made to ensure that the necessary information from various departments was systematically collected, rendering infrequent all-out efforts unnecessary.

3.6   Several-leveled Flowchart

The chart in Figure 3.5 is perhaps not a good example, but if the process to start with is long and complex, or much other information is added to a flowchart, it might easily become difficult to read. This can be remedied by breaking it down into several hierarchical levels, both for ordinary and cross-functional flowcharts (Andersen and Pettersen, 1996).

The principle is that on the top level, only the main activities are shown. These are numbered 1.0, 2.0, and so on. This top level gives a good overview of the entire process without blurring the major aspects with many details. Figure 3.7 shows a somewhat simplified version of the chart in Figure 3.5 as a level 0-chart.

For each of the main activities to be presented in more detail, another flowchart on the level below this one is created. For activity 3.0, the more detailed chart is shown in Figure 3.8. The individual steps at this level are logically linked to the level above by numbering them 3.1, 3.2, and so on. If there is a need for further detailing, more levels are simply added. By using this technique, it is possible to present the overall process using only a level 0-chart. As the need occurs, details are displayed for the individual steps of the process through lower level charts. This makes the technique very powerful through combining a lucid presentation format with details, where needed.

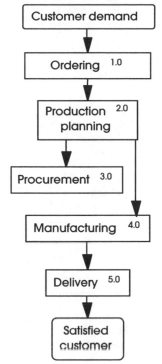

Figure 3.7. Level 0-chart for the process.

To ensure that all departments used the same procedure for storing the necessary information for financial reporting, the company from the last example decided to document the ideal information flow of the process by using several-leveled flowcharts. The flowchart in the previous example, Figure 3.6, constituted the level 0-chart, and the step that represented the activity taking place in all departments was termed 4.0. As the reporting required different information from different departments, department-specific procedures were produced at level 1. For the procurement department, the chart is shown in Figure 3.9.

3.7 Paper-and-Pencil or PC?

A highly relevant question related to process documentation and drawing flowcharts is what medium should be used. Is it better to stick to the old tools of paper and pencil or be more up-to-date and draw on a PC? As for many other questions, the answer for this one is both.

In the first phase, trying to agree on how the process truly looks, it is definitely an advantage to use paper. In the type of plenary sessions common in this phase, a flip chart or other type of large sheets to hang on the wall should be used. Usually, many opinions surface and the flowchart will be a dynamic representation that is constantly changing. A technique that enables quite painless adjustments to these dynamics is using colored "Post It" notes or other pieces of paper with glue for representing

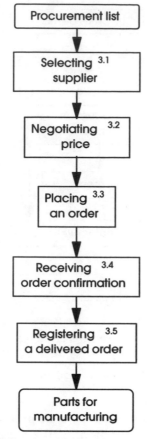

Figure 3.8. Level 1-chart for procurement.

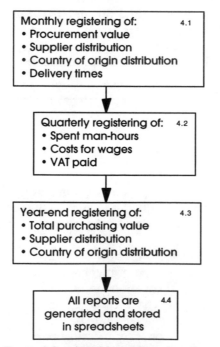

Figure 3.9. Level 1-chart for reporting.

process elements. As the chart is being developed, the notes can be moved around and the bother of erasing and redrawing is avoided.

For this purpose, a computer is of comparatively little use. First of all, the screen is too small. Even if it is enlarged by using an overhead projector, it is still awkward working on a PC in this type of meeting. Furthermore, from experience, there is always a danger that the software tool itself takes attention away from the process and the documentation task.

In the next round, however, it is necessary to capture the flowchart from the less manageable, large format used during the development of it. The flowchart must be stored, copied, and modified. For these purposes, the computer is clearly highly suitable. There are a number of software tools available on the market that make the construction and adjustment of flowcharts very easy. The price is usually not frightening; $200 to $300 dollars buys a powerful tool. Two of the more easy-to-use programs tested by the author are Visio Professional and Micrografx's FlowCharter.

After the flowchart has been completed, but also between meetings during the process, the flowchart is drawn using a PC. The chart can then be printed and copied for distributing. In addition, the file itself can be sent across large distances—for example, by e-mail—to others who might need the chart (for instance, benchmarking partners). The software allows the user to update the chart as new meetings are being held. Afterwards, the chart can be stored electronically and updated and changed as the business process changes over time. It is difficult and bothersome doing this maintenance by hand, as it involves a lot of erasing and changing each time the chart is being updated. Such a two-step approach, where the most suitable media for different purposes are used, is by far more favorable than categorically selecting one or the other for the entire job.

3.8 Process Ownership

Many organizations initiate their change to process orientation in one of the ways outlined so far—that is, either through a complete documentation of all business processes at once, or by a gradual documentation as new improvement projects are launched. No matter how this is solved practically, it can be useful to introduce the term *process ownership* in the organization. A normal problem in organizations that are still focusing on departments or have just started to orient themselves toward business processes, is that very few people feel responsible for the organization's processes. There are usually limited definitions of where one process ends and the next one starts; no one has been given the responsibility for delivering the product from the process to the customer—internally or externally—on time, and of the right quality. At best, someone assumes responsibility for the process, but then often more than one person does so simultaneously. The result is that local "emperors" can be found around the organization, ruling over segments of the process, but without having anyone possessing the complete responsibility for the entire process. A distinguishing feature of processes without ownership is that no improvements are initiated unless there exists a clear order from management to do so.

The introduction of process ownership—that is, appointing individuals as owners of the individual business processes of the enterprise—is an attempt to remedy this situation. Either before documenting a process or by selecting one from the group of people who already performed this task, one person is given the responsibility for the process. The appointing must be done by management. A general rule is that the person involved in the process with the highest organizational authority or impacts the largest portion of the process, should become process owner. This responsibility includes:

- That the process owner is given the necessary authority to initiate changes to the process.

- That the process owner is responsible for continuously measuring the performance level of the process.

- That the process owner is responsible for initiating improvements to the process.

- That the process owner must establish some type of steering group for the process that will work together to improve it. This steering group will normally consist of persons who perform tasks within the process, but suppliers and customers of the process are also relevant members.

After having introduced process orientation and process ownership, the organizational chart will change character, from consisting of vertical silos with department managers to horizontal processes with process owners. Examples of the two extremes are shown in Figure 3.10 and Figure 3.11.

It should also be pointed out that often there will be a hierarchy of business processes and corresponding process owners. As can be seen in Figure 3.11, the extensive process of *manufacturing and delivery of products to customers* has one process owner coordinating high-level issues related to this process. At the same time, this process consists of several "shorter" processes at the level below—for example, *order handling, manufacturing*, and *delivery and installation*. The individual process owners for these subprocesses are responsible for their isolated processes, but must coordinate their activity with the process owner of the overall process. As was mentioned, the process owners have the overall responsibility for carrying out improvements in their processes, but such initiatives must obviously also be coordinated with the management and the overall organization-wide improvement planning to avoid conflicting actions.

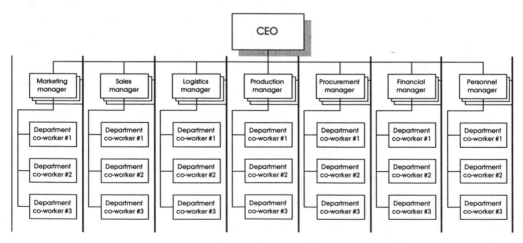

Figure 3.10. Traditional organization with vertical silos.

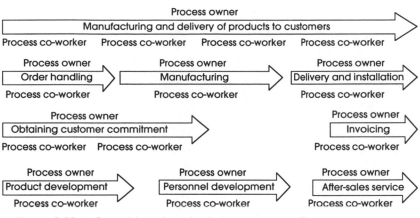

Figure 3.11.   Organizing along business processes with process owners.

REFERENCES

Andersen, Bjørn, and Per-Gaute Pettersen. *The Benchmarking Handbook: Step-by-Step Instructions.* Chapman & Hall, London, England, 1996.

Peppard, Joe. "Benchmarking Business Process: A Framework and Classification Scheme." *In* Proceedings of the ESPRIT–COPERNICUS Symposium, *Distributed Enterprise, Intelligent Automation, and Industrial Benchmarking.* Wroclaw, Poland, 1998.

CHAPTER 4

Performance Measurement

One argument for the importance of process documentation was that to improve something, you needed to know the current state of things. Correspondingly, the general argument for performance measurement is that to improve a process, you must know how well it is performing today. This chapter will give a brief overview over the most important principles of performance measurement.

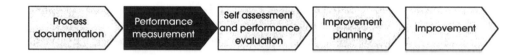

4.1 What is Performance Measurement and Why Measure?

Quite generally, all management and decision-making are highly dependent on information about status and development over time. Measurement is an important part of this. When discussing improvement of business processes, measuring the processes' performance levels is an important and necessary element. Performance measurement provides information about how well a process is being conducted and how good the results from it are. Having relevant performance measures for the organization's business processes is important to know where you are today, which in turn enables you to:

- Identify processes or areas that need improvement.

- Form an impression of the development over time—that is, the trend of the performance.

- Compare your own performance level against that of others.

- Assess whether improvement projects started (and possibly completed) really have or will produce results.

- Based on this, evaluate what improvement tools should be used in the future.

An insightful statement is:

> *"You cannot manage what you cannot measure."*

Related points about measurement are:

- What gets measured, gets done—that is, areas emphasized through monitoring and measurement also receive attention and resources.

- Measurement impacts behavior—that is, initiating measurement often creates changes in the behavior of the system to accommodate the measuring.

As previously mentioned, companies have traditionally been divided into functional departments. In addition, the dominant dimension in performance monitoring has been financial parameters, often taken directly from the accounting systems. The problem is that such measures have often been in direct conflict with improvement and have hampered actions directed at such. The fact is that for many improvement efforts, it can be very difficult to justify them through a regular investment analysis. Usually, expenses are necessary for both training and carrying out the project. The improvements, on the other hand, are often of a more operational character (for example, reduced times, reduced defect rates, and so on). These can be quite challenging to quantify in a financial language, and can appear only after some time—that is, in the future. It is therefore difficult to get approval for spending the necessary resources and time in improvement projects.

In recent years, the development has been directed toward more operational systems for performance measurement. It is, however, beyond the scope of this book to deal with performance measurement in general and in an extensive manner. To support the improvement approach described here, it is, however, necessary to develop a system that contains the following elements:

- Continuous measurement of relevant aspects of the performance of the main business processes, perhaps 15 to 30 processes. What is meant by "relevant aspects" is treated later in this chapter.

- These measurements must together form a complete and overall instrument panel that can be used for monitoring the performance. In opposition to the typical financial instrument panel, which consists of the lagging red warning lamp for profit/deficit, this panel will contain a number of gages that display actual status (see Figure 4.1).

Financial indicator

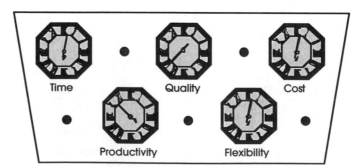

Operational instrument panel

Figure 4.1.   Different measurement systems.

- The instrument panel will expose any occurring negative trends, generally show the development over time, and enable following up specific improvement efforts.

Care should be taken, however, not to measure too much. . . .

Xerox in the United States and Rank Xerox in Europe have internationally been at the front in the development of operational performance measurement. However, this went so far that something of a joke in the corporation became, "If it moves, measure it!" The result was, of course, that so much information was produced that no one neither had any use for it nor even had the time to look at it. Thus, all information was disregarded, including that which was truly important, and the entire measurement effort worked directly against its purpose.

To conclude this section, some "established truths" about measurement will be presented, which today at best must be seen as *variations* of the truth:

- *Measurement is threatening!* Measurement has for a long time, especially in the era initiated by Taylor and his time and motion studies, been focused on controlling the employees. The kind of measurement advocated in this book has a totally different purpose—that is, to form an impression of how well processes work, not to find scapegoats. Another point to be made is that measurement and evaluation must be separated. Measurement has in itself never been threatening to anyone; it is the ensuing interpretation and use of the measurement results that have been negatively directed.

- *Precision is essential for useful measurement!* This might be true for very technical measurement or even for accounting purposes, but not for operational performance measurement. The purpose of the performance measurement is to indicate whether improvements are achieved or not, not the exact performance level. Putting too many resources into developing painstakingly precise and accurate measurement systems can actually delay and obstruct the introduction of a practical system that works. A somewhat more pragmatic attitude is required in this respect.

- *Subjective measures are sloppy!* The traditional "accounting view" of the world, that is, that money is the only reliable measure—has obstructed the use of softer dimensions in measurement systems. Parameters like the quality of the working situation, the product's ability to satisfy needs, and so on, do, however, provide valuable information and should not be rejected because they cannot be translated into monetary figures.

- *Standards are necessary!* On the contrary, standards often function as a ceiling for the performance level. People have a tendency to view standards as an upper limit for the performance. Well-defined standards imply that as long as you stay within them, there is no need for improvement.

4.2   Types of Performance Measures

With regard to specific performance measures defined for the measurement of performance levels, it is important to be aware of the differences between certain characteristics of measures.

"Hard" versus "soft" measures

"Hard" measures are pure facts that can be measured directly, while "soft" measures are less tangible conditions that must be measured indirectly. Another set of terms is "quantitative" measures and "qualitative" measures. The time it takes to carry out something or how much it costs, are typical hard measures. Quality, expressed as satisfaction of needs or attitudes, is one example of a typical soft measure. Some differences between hard and soft measures are listed in Table 4.1.

Hard measures are by far more widely used; soft measures are seen by many as being so inaccurate that they are rarely useful. On the other hand, as Deming (1986) underlined, the most important numbers are often not known. Management by numbers is one of the deadly diseases that have ruined many enterprises in the Western world. Customer satisfaction is a good example of a soft performance measure that is best expressed as the customers' attitudes toward the product or service being delivered. In fear of this being too difficult to measure accurately, many companies have tried to define customer satisfaction as the number of complaints or warranty costs. To assume that those who do not complain are satisfied is at best naïve, at worst completely wrong. The conclusion is that both hard *and* soft measures are necessary to give a complete picture.

Hard measures	Soft measures
Objective reference	Observer bias
Accurately known	Surrogate indicator
Hierarchical	Multivariable situation

Table 4.1.   Differences between hard and soft measures.

In many cases, when trying to measure softer dimensions of performance, it is necessary to approach the problem through the use of so-called surrogate indicators. If, for example, there is a need to measure the soft measure of quality of the atmosphere in a meeting room, this can be quite difficult. It is possible to measure specific conditions like temperature, humidity, and air circulation. The problem with these measures is that no optimal value can be easily defined, as this will depend heavily on the individual participants in the meeting. Some surrogate indicators that can be used in this case are:

- **The number of persons active in the discussion**
- **The number of ideas or suggestions generated**

- **The number of persons leaving the room for various reasons**

Even if they are not direct translations of what was originally attempted measure, such indicators can give indirect interpretations about the performance level of it.

Financial versus nonfinancial measures

Financial measures include both basic and derived measures of financial character and/or using monetary values as the measurement unit. Such measures are almost always hard, but are usually the result of some type of calculations. A few such measures are shown in Table 4.2.

Focusing on such financial measures is obviously an important part of the traditional way of running and managing a business. Financial measures were often seen as synonymous with performance due to the direct link to the company's financial result. The increasing understanding that competitive advantage is more closely linked to operational conditions like delivery time, delivery precision, and quality, has often been met with a redefinition of such operative dimensions to financially based indicators.

The term *nonfinancial measures* is a common denominator for performance measures that have measurement units other than monetary value. They can be both hard and soft, as shown in the examples below:

- Set-up time
- Delivery time
- Delivery precision
- Defect rate
- Number of complaints
- Customer satisfaction
- Quality of work life

As for hard and soft measures, the conclusion with regard to financial and nonfinancial measures is that both are needed. Problems arise when one of the categories is left out of the equation.

Financial measure	Calculation (simplified)
Profit margin	Total sales – Total costs
Value added	Sales – Input goods
Turnover of capital	Sales/Total capital

Table 4.2. Examples of financial measures.

Result versus process measures

These are not necessarily conflicting concepts, but rather two types of measures that also should act in a balanced interplay. These two dimensions are, by the way, often used to illustrate the differences between Western and Japanese thinking when it comes to management. Western management culture emphasizes results and measure accordingly—that is, using measurement systems focused on measuring achievements.

In line with the traditional Japanese attitudes, the most important part is performing the process in a respectable manner, which will in turn give the desired results. This is reflected in the Japanese measurement systems, where far more emphasis is put on so-called *process measures*—measures that describe certain important characteristics of a process and that are assumed to have an effect on the desired results. An example can be the number of meetings held in a cross-functional team; the typical corresponding Western measure would be the number of changes implemented.

A manager of a large agricultural collective in the former Soviet Union three years in a row won the prize for the most productive collective. The performance measure used was the number of kilos of meat produced per year. The fourth year, he shot himself. He had no breeding stock left.

Measures defined according to purpose

A different way of classifying the types of performance measures is through the purpose of the measures—that is, what they are supposed to say something about. Three common categories are:

- Result measures
- Diagnostic measures
- Competence measures

Result measures are, as previously mentioned, measures that say something about what the organization achieves. Some typical examples are:

- Net profit
- Return on investments
- Market share

These measures say something about what results were achieved in the preceding period. They do, however, say little about how they were achieved and if this state will continue. In this way, they are lagging measures. Imagine, for instance, a company that realizes that profits are sinking and therefore cuts investments to reduce expenses. Another company experiences the same, but continues to invest to become more competitive. Which company has the higher performance level? This simple example shows the dangers of focusing too strongly on result measures.

Diagnostic measures are indicators of future results and can be viewed as indirect measures of achievement. They represent typical critical success factors for the organization and are not necessarily linked to financial aspects. The term "diagnostic" is inspired by health care, where diagnosis is a determination of an ailment's nature and means for curing it. This way, diagnostic measures are supposed to say something about an organization's health and possible ways to improve it. They are a central part of a system for early warning that will alert management about a negative development. Typical measures are:

- Delivery precision
- Delivery flexibility
- Product quality
- Lead times
- Customer satisfaction

Diagnostic measures are often operational, but are assumed to have a high impact on the future financial results.

The third type of measure, *competence measure*, is the hardest one to define, but is introduced to enable determining in advance whether the organization is capable of adjusting to future changes in requirements posed. Being "capable" means having the competencies, personnel, and abilities needed to do what must be done, both today and tomorrow. Competence measures are thus related to the ability to change. Some possible measures are:

- Investments in product development
- Attitudes toward change
- Flexibility to manufacture totally new products or deliver totally new services
- Training levels

These three categories of measures have a different validity horizon. As shown in Figure 4.2 (Bredrup, 1995), result measures are really measures that are most valid for saying something about the past. Diagnostic measures are relevant for the immediate future; competence measures are generally hard to define in a way that offers high validity, but the objective is that should be able to say something about both the short- and long-term future.

4.3   The Contents of the Instrument Panel

As mentioned earlier in this chapter, the objective of the work of creating a performance measurement system should be to create an instrument panel that shows the performance level of the organization's main business processes. It is unfortunately not possible in a book like this to describe exactly which "instruments" or gages the individual organization should include in this panel. As a part of several international research projects, it has been attempted to define a common set of performance measures that are supposed to be general and to be used by any organization. It has, however, proven difficult to accomplish this task, and it is probably not preferable either.

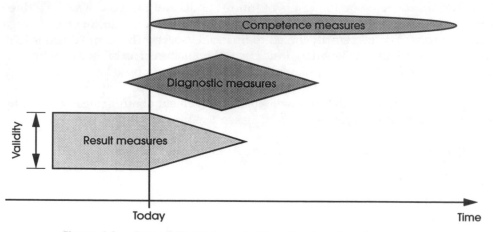

Figure 4.2.   The validity horizon of different categories of measures.

Instead, the individual organization should on its own define the business processes believed to be the most important ones, how these should be measured, and how often.

The descriptions of the different classes of performance measures should be used as a starting point for defining these issues. Please also remember that a balanced instrument panel that measures hard and soft, financial and nonfinancial, and result and process measures, is important. As a last guideline, it is worth keeping in mind that for each process, most of the following main dimensions should be covered:

- Time, as speed with regard to delivery, execution, and so on, is becoming more and more important (Stalk and Hout, 1990).

- Quality, measured either as the more specific factor of defect rate, but also as the product's or service's ability to satisfy needs and expectation.

- Cost, as one important dimension of the performance picture, but not the entire picture, as it has traditionally been.

- Flexibility, which is also a dimension of growing importance, for example, expressed as customer-adaptation of products.

- Environmental impact, which is a somewhat unusual dimension in this respect, but one that is also becoming crucial when discussing the overall performance of an organization.

In addition to the framework of business processes developed in the ENAPS project, as shown in Figure 1.3, a set of performance indicators for these processes has also been developed. As this set is quite extensive, it has been placed in the Appendix, where the reader might find valuable hints for useful measures. Please do not use the ENAPS measures directly, but try to adapt them to suit the individual organization's characteristic features.

REFERENCES

Bredrup, Harald. "Performance Measurement in a Changing Competitive Industrial Environment: Breaking the Financial Paradigm." Ph.D. Thesis, Norwegian Institute of Technology, Trondheim, Norway, 1995.

Deming, W. Edwards. *Out of the Crisis: Quality, Productivity and Competitive Position.* Cambridge University Press, Cambridge, Massachusetts, USA, 1986.

Stalk, George Jr., and Thomas M. Hout. *Competing Against Time: How Time-Based Competition Is Reshaping Global Markets.* The Free Press, New York City, New York, USA, 1990.

CHAPTER 5

Self Assessment and Improvement Planning

Before commencing an improvement process, it is important to know where the need for improvement is highest. A tool for conducting an analysis of this question is self assessment, which combines process documentation with performance measurement. This chapter describes self assessment and how to perform one. Furthermore, it is explained how the results from the self assessment can be used for an ensuing planning of the improvement effort.

5.1 Definition of Self Assessment

Self assessment is a technique for evaluating the performance level of an organization and its processes. The word *self* separates the evaluation from an evaluation conducted by an external third party—that is, the organization performs the evaluation itself. From this definition, self assessment sounds much like an ordinary performance measurement system. What, then, separates a "normal" performance measurement system from self assessment? The line is probably not crystal clear, but some differences are (Rolstadås, 1995):

- *The time of measurement.* While measuring continuously in a measurement system, self assessment is conducted only at a few moments in time with a certain period between each self assessment.

- *Focus.* While an ordinary measurement system provides rather detailed measurements within single processes, the purpose of self assessment is to give a more overall and coherent picture of the organization's performance.

- *Use.* Data from the ordinary measurement system is used more for the day-to-day running of the processes and monitoring of improvements. Self assessment results are to a higher extent used for defining more long-term focus areas for improvement and as strategic decision support.

Summarized, it can be said that measurement by self assessment is at a more coherent and overall strategic level and is conducted at a lower frequency. In the improvement process advocated in this book, self assessment constitutes a logical first activity. This serves several purposes:

- To conduct a self assessment, the organization's business processes must first be documented.

- Performance measures for the processes must also be developed—that is, by planning to carry out a self assessment, the organization is forced to undertake these two introductory and highly important tasks.

- Most importantly, the self assessment provides management with an overview of improvement needs and potential, thus enabling the directing of improvement resources toward the right area or process.

5.2   Developing a System for Self Assessment

There are, in fact, different types of self assessment. In recent years, many organizations started conducting self assessment based on the criteria of quality awards like The Malcolm Baldrige National Quality and the European Quality Award from the European Foundation for Quality Management. Criteria for evaluation in these awards are more or less defined along process independent dimensions. Another approach builds on measurement at the process level. In line with the process-orientation that forms the framework for this book, the last approach is described here.

The performance measures used in a self assessment should be of a different nature than those in the ordinary measurement system. While a measurement system is designed to display the detailed performance level of the organization's business processes, the purpose of the self assessment is to give a more coarse overview over which processes are working satisfactorily and which should be improved. The measures of the self assessment should therefore be on a higher level and cover complete business processes.

When developing a system for self assessment, it is usually possible to discern two distinct phases (Rolstadås, 1995):

1. Development of a first version.

2. Adjustments and preventive maintenance during use of the system.

When developing the system, the main challenges are often:

1. Defining the organization's core processes and deciding which of these should be covered by the self assessment. A logical number of processes would be between ten and twenty that are of high importance for the organization's competitiveness, typically processes like product development, delivery, service provision, procurement, and so on.

2. Linking performance measures to these core processes, preferably variations over the five main dimensions described in chapter 4. If one of the processes in the self assessment is product development, obvious performance measures could be the number of products developed during a certain period of time, the costs for developing a standard product, and market impact.

3. Determining the time intervals for conducting the self assessment. A logical frequency is once per six months, but this can be increased or decreased according to needs.

These three elements—the business processes, the performance measures, and a plan for conducting the analysis—constitute the core of the system for self assessment.

Once the system has been developed, self assessments must be carried out according to the defined plan. The collected information—that is, the measurements—must be stored for enabling comparisons across time and identifying trends in the performance. Based on the information from the self assessment, areas that need improvement can be determined, strengths be identified that can be used as competitive advantage, and so on. This information is used for prioritizing improvement areas and planning the improvement activity for the next period. By supplementing the self assessment information with data from external benchmarking, another dimension can be added to the assessments by including external reference points.

It is important, however, that the system is maintained to keep, and even to improve, its ability to conduct correct and valuable assessments. The need for adjustments to the system arises as a consequence of experience from using the self assessment and changing conditions surrounding the organization. The maintenance consists of a more defensive adjustment of parts of the system that are obviously obsolete—for example, removing processes that are no longer performed by the organization. Even more important is a more proactive development of the system to give even more valuable information—that is, changing the focus of the measurements to areas expected to become more vital in the future. There is, however, a potential conflict between the desire for changing the system and the need for stability of the measures used. Without a certain degree of continuity, comparisons against previous measurements will be meaningless.

5.3   Interpreting the Measurements

Conducting the self assessment—that is, the pure measurement part—is one thing. If the self assessment is to be useful, interpretation of the results must be performed after the measurements have been done. Without interpretation, the measurements themselves have little value.

When it comes to making use of the self assessment results for prioritizing improvement efforts, there are three especially useful tools:

- Trend analysis

- Spider chart

- Performance matrix

Each of these contributes in its own way to better insight into the overall performance of the organization and where improvements are needed.

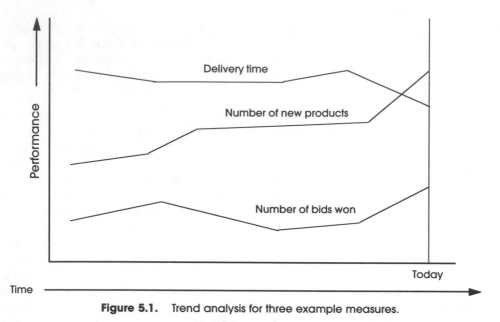

Figure 5.1.   Trend analysis for three example measures.

5.3.1 Trend Analysis

Trend analysis is, as the name implies, simply an analysis of the development of the performance level. By comparing the last measurement with previous measurements, it is possible to form an opinion of the direction of the development. Figure 5.1 shows a simple diagram that can be used to graphically portray this information. In this diagram, three measures have been included, but it is possible to use one diagram for each measure, or include all measures for a business process in one diagram.

Measures that display a negative trend will obviously be relevant candidates for improvement. As will be demonstrated a little later, however, it is not only the development over time that impacts this decision, but also how important the business process is for the competitiveness of the organization.

A medium-sized American company that strongly emphasized both product development and efficient manufacturing of goods, mainly for exporting to Europe, had been conducting performance measurement for quite some time. The company still did not feel certain that the measurements gave a correct picture of the situation. Central performance measures had traditionally been:

- Manufacturing costs per unit, both for components and for finished products, measured as the total running costs for machinery and equipment divided by the number of manufactured units. This measure had, in previous years, shown a steady increase, and much effort had been put into reducing it.

- The costs for purchased parts present in the end product. This measure had also been increasing, and many suppliers had been replaced, without giving the desired results.

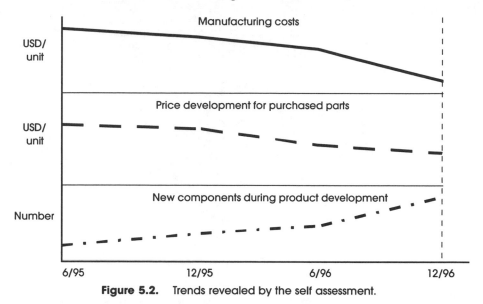

Figure 5.2.   Trends revealed by the self assessment.

The company hired external assistance for designing a system for self assessment every six months. Some important performance measures in the self assessment were:

- True manufacturing costs per unit, measured as the manufacturing time multiplied by an hourly rate for the machine or equipment in question.
- Price development for purchased parts.
- The number of new components specified during product development.

A trend analysis of these measures after two years of measurement showed a completely different situation, as shown in Figure 5.2.

It appeared that the total volume, expressed as the number of products, had decreased somewhat, as one product now could perform more than one function. Thus, the total running costs for the manufacturing equipment had been divided by fewer units, which resulted in the believed increase in manufacturing costs. The fact was that regular improvements in this process had given a continuous decrease in the costs. At the same time, the old performance measure of price development for purchased components had increased due to a change in the product developers' practice, to using more purchased parts in the products. In fact, the prices for comparable components had been reduced continuously. An important reason why the manufacturing costs and the prices for purchased parts had not decreased even more was the continuous introduction of new components during product development. All these matters were revealed through the self assessment, and the improvement effort was directed toward the product development process.

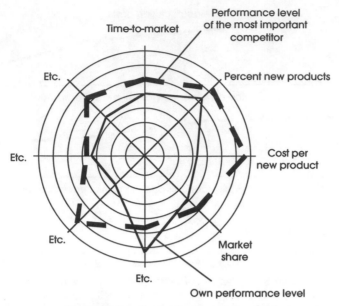

Figure 5.3.   Example of a spider chart.

5.3.2 Spider Chart

While the trend analysis renders it possible to compare the current performance level to previous measurements, the spider chart is a tool for comparing the organization's own performance level to that of other organizations (Andersen and Pettersen, 1996). By using the spider chart, the results from the self assessment can be interpreted in relation to other enterprises—for example, competitors.

Figure 5.3 shows an example of a spider chart for the business process of product development. Each spoke in the chart represents one performance measure for this process. It is also possible to use one chart for the entire organization and let the spokes represent processes. The performance level is indicated by plotting a point on the spoke, where the performance level increases with increasing radius. The farther from the center of the chart the point is placed, the better the performance. For each spoke, the relevant unit of measurement for the performance level is used. This gives different units of measurement for the individual spokes, but does not cause any problems. The main purpose is to create some type of a performance profile, which is done by drawing lines between the points in the chart.

By plotting the performance level of both our own organization and the level of one or more other organizations, an image is formed of how good we are ourselves. Input for constructing the chart will typically be market analyses, industry statistics, and the like. Depending on where the gap to the competitors is largest, you can select the business processes that should be improved.

After realizing where improvements were needed, the company in the previous example wanted to compare that status to their competitors. Through gathering information from different sources, including brochures and statistics from the competitors themselves, a spider chart for comparison was drawn. The result is shown in Figure 5.4.

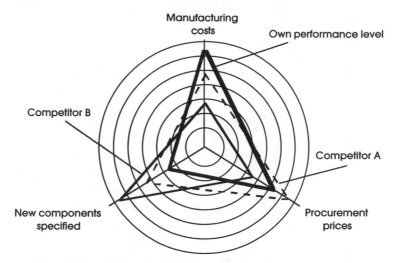

Figure 5.4.   Spider chart for the central performance measures.

This confirmed that the efforts to reduce the manufacturing costs had given results, but that there was still a potential with regard to procurement prices, perhaps by entering into more long-term relationships with a few suppliers. Furthermore, this showed that the performance level pertaining to standardization of components in new products was dismal. It was thus correct to start improvement initiatives within this process.

5.3.3 Performance Matrix

The performance matrix is used to analyze not only how well the organization's business processes are performed, but also how important they are perceived to be (Andersen and Pettersen, 1996). This supplements the two preceding tools, which focus on performance alone. By using the performance matrix as well, the organization can avoid using resources to improve processes that are not performing satisfactorily, but that are not very important either.

An example of a performance matrix is shown in Figure 5.5. The matrix is divided into quadrants, placing *importance* along the horizontal axis and the *current performance* level along the vertical. The individual processes are plotted in the matrix based on the measurements from the self assessment and an evaluation of their importance. The meaning of each quadrant follows:

- *Unimportant* (low importance, low performance): The performance level is, true enough, low, but the low importance renders it unnecessary to put any resources into improvement.

- *Overkill* (low importance, high performance): The performance level is high, but this is of less consequence because the business processes in this quadrant are not especially important for the organization's competitiveness. This is thus no candidate for improvement.

- *Must be improved* (high importance, low performance): This is the obvious area for starting improvements. The business processes that fall within this area are important, while the current performance level is low.

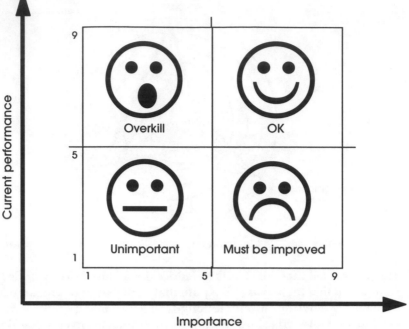

Figure 5.5.   Example of a performance matrix.

- *OK* (high importance, high performance): A golden rule is that areas where the performance is already good, should also be improved. However, the business processes that in addition to being important are not being performed well today (*Must be improved*), should be improved first. If no processes fall within this quadrant, processes in the OK quadrant can be relevant candidates for improvement efforts.

A manufacturer of heavy mechanical equipment for marine applications had identified six critical issues measured through self assessment. All measures showed a potential for improvement, but there were not sufficient resources to start with all six of them at once. The company found it difficult to decide where to start the improvement activity. To prioritize, a performance matrix was constructed that included the following six measures:

1. **Advanced and flexible product design**

2. **Delivery time**

3. **Delivery precision**

4. **Price**

5. **Accessibility for maintenance and repairs**

6. **Product design and finish**

The matrix in Figure 5.6 helped the company decide to concentrate on improving the delivery time and delivery precision.

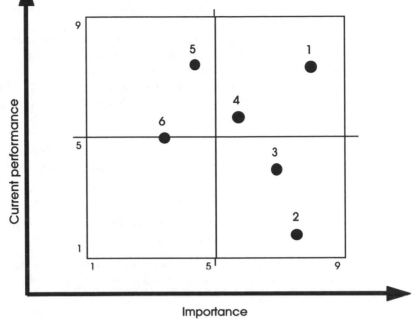

Figure 5.6.   Performance matrix for the six performance measures.

A balanced use of these three tools after having conducted a self assessment should give a clear indication of which business processes should be concentrated on during the next period. This result can very well be summarized in a priority list that will give guidelines for improvement efforts ahead. As processes on the list are improved or a new self assessment is performed, the list is updated. Two other tools, criteria testing and Quality Function Deployment (QFD), can also be used to supplement the decision-support for directing the improvement resources in the right direction.

5.4   Criteria Testing

If the organization has a clear perception of what major factors its competitiveness is based on, criteria testing is a tool that can be used for numerically analyzing which business processes have the highest impact on these factors (Andersen and Pettersen, 1996). The tool is therefore well suited for changing the focus from so-called *critical success factors* (CSF) to business processes, but still allows the improvement efforts to be directed at the processes that really impact competitiveness.

Before the tool itself is presented, the term *critical success factor* should be defined. One possible definition is:

> *A limited number of factors that to a large extent impacts the organization's competitiveness and its performance in the marketplace.*

Typical examples of such critical success factors are the price asked for the organization's products or services, the quality of the same, special features of the products or services, and so on. If asking the question, "What is it that our customers truly value about our enterprise and help maintain them as customers?", the answer will usually constitute the critical success factors.

If however, one, tries to improve these directly to increase the competitiveness, it can be difficult determining where to concentrate the efforts. If delivery precision is the enterprise's main competitive advantage, for example, it is likely not obvious what causes this and how it can be improved. Criteria testing is a matrix-based tool that assists in determining this. A typical form used for criteria testing is shown in Figure 5.7.

The procedure for using criteria testing is as follows:

1. Place the identified critical success factors, typically a number from three to five, in the upper field of the matrix. If desired, assign each of these a different weight factor that expresses relative importance. In Figure 5.7, weight factors from 1 to 3 are used, but other numeric values can be used as well.

2. Next, place in the left-hand field of the matrix all possible business processes assumed to have an impact on these factors.

3. Assess for each business process its impact on each of the critical success factors. Again, the example uses impact factors from 1 to 3, where 1 means low impact and 3 high impact.

4. Multiply the impact factor by the weight factor of the critical success factor, and place the product in the matrix cells.

5. For each business process, these products are summarized horizontally and the total sum placed in the right-hand column of the matrix. This numeric value indicates the collective impact of the business process on the complete set of critical success factors. The higher the score, the better reason to improve this process, as this will give the highest overall effect on the organization's critical success factors.

Processes	CSF / Weight	1 / 3	2 / 1	3 / 1	4 / 3	5 / 2	Total score
Process 1		3	1	2	9	4	19
Process 2		9	3	1	3	2	18
Process 3		9	2	3	6	6	(26)
.							
.							
.							
.							
.							
.							
Process *n*		3	2	2	3	6	16

Figure 5.7. Matrix for criteria testing.

It should also be pointed out that the assessments made during the criteria testing, both to assign weight factors and to determine the impact factors, are quite subjective. The numeric values obtained at the end of the test should thus only be viewed as directional, and not as absolute answers. The more persons that participate in the test, the more valid the results must be assumed to be.

A chain of hair stylists for both men and women initiated an improvement project to rectify its decreasing sales over a long period. The following critical success factors were identified:

1. Price was important, but only as long as it was in line with that of competing salons.

2. Good appointment availability—that is, the possibility of getting an appointment at the desired time.

3. The possibility for establishing a customer–stylist relationship. Because of some recent changes in the staff, this had been difficult over the past two years, which the customers had reacted negatively to.

4. Additional services, such as solarium, and manicure, as requested by many customers.

These factors were assigned weight factors and a criteria testing was performed. The result is displayed in Figure 5.8. The conclusion was to concentrate the effort around the three processes that ended up with the highest scores:, recruiting, time planning, and accepting appointment reservations.

Business processes	CSF / Weight	1 / 1	2 / 3	3 / 3	4 / 2	Total score
Haircut and other services		3	3	0	0	6
Time planning		1	9	6	0	(16)
Accepting reservations		0	9	6	0	(15)
Recruiting		1	3	9	6	(19)
Keeping the staff		1	0	9	0	10
Planning additional services		0	0	0	6	6
Purchasing accessories		3	0	0	2	5

Figure 5.8.   Criteria testing for a hair stylist's chain.

5.5   Improvement Planning Using QFD

The Quality Function Deployment tool, QFD, was developed to represent a customer-oriented approach to product development. For this usage, it is a methodology for structuring customer needs, expectations, and requirements, and translating these into detailed product and process specifications. The principles can, however, also be used for a number of other problems, including improvement planning.

5.5.1 The Theory behind QFD

Before showing how QFD can be applied to improvement planning, the basic theory behind the tool is presented. To start with, the product development process consists of several sequential phases (Akao, 1990):

- Transforming customer requirements into a product concept

- Transforming the product concept into a product design

- Transforming the product design into a process design

- Transforming the process design into production documents

Each step of this process must adhere to the original customer requirements. The basic structure of QFD is a relational matrix at different stages of the process, as shown in Figure 5.9.

WHAT constitutes the goals of the analysis, which in the case of the first phase of product development is the customer requirements and expectations. HOW expresses the means to reach these goals, in the product development's first phase being technical product concepts. In the next phase, these will form the WHATs, and HOW will represent detailed design solutions for the product concept. If a weight factor for each

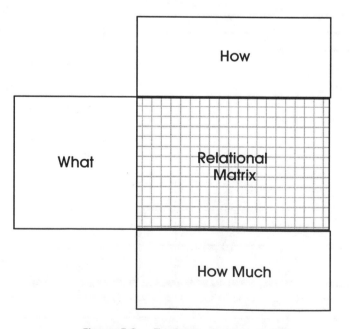

Figure 5.9.   The basic structure of QFD.

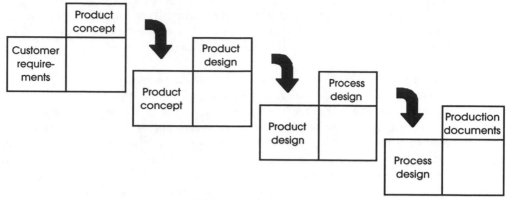

Figure 5.10. A chain of QFD charts.

element of WHAT is multiplied by a grade indicating how well each element of HOW contributes to satisfying the requirement, an indicator for the performance of each HOW element is generated, which is placed in the field HOW MUCH. This way, each phase of the product development process is linked together as a chain of relational matrices, as shown Figure 5.10, to ensure that the voice of the customer is transmitted throughout the entire process.

Additional information can also be added, thus creating the chart popularly known as the "house of quality" as shown in Figure 5.11.

The QFD process is conducted by entering data into each room of the house of quality. As was mentioned, WHAT represents the external requirements, in product development the customer's product requirements. To each element in WHAT is attached a weight factor expressing the element's importance, which renders it possible to emphasize some requirements more strongly than others. WHY represents the

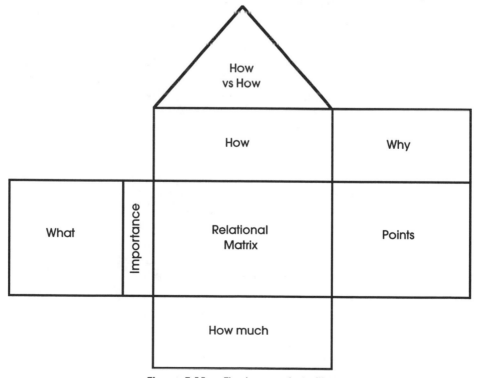

Figure 5.11. The house of quality.

challenges facing the organization—for example, competitors' solutions to these customer requirements. This can be expressed through a type of benchmarking of different competitors' offers and their quality or performance. An example is shown in Figure 5.12.

After determining how the customer requirements can be fulfilled—that is, HOW—the relational matrix linking WHAT and HOW is completed. To make the matrix as clear as possible, it is usually preferable to use as few types of relations as possible. A set of commonly used symbols is shown in Figure 5.13. In the same manner, the roof of the house of quality forms a relational matrix to be used for investigating whether there are any relationships among the different elements of HOW. In this matrix, it is possible to indicate both positive and negative relations—that is, factors that work together or that create trade-offs or conflicts. Some common symbols for this matrix are shown Figure 5.14. For each HOW, the weight for the determined relationship to the individual element of WHAT is multiplied by the corresponding factor for importance for each requirement element. All products are summarized and placed in the lower field of the chart, HOW MUCH. Elements of HOW with a high

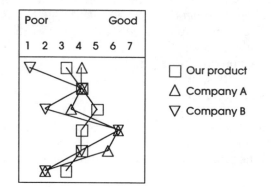

Figure 5.12.   Benchmarking of others' offers.

Relation	Symbol	Weight
Weak	△	1
Medium	○	3
Strong	◉	9

Figure 5.13.   Symbols for the relational matrix.

Relationship	Symbol
Strong positive	◉
Weak positive	○
Weak negative	✕
Strong negative	✖

Figure 5.14.   Symbols for the roof matrix.

score in this field should be preferred to others if all elements cannot be incorporated into the product.

5.5.2 QFD as a Tool for improvement

QFD is a technique that is useful for ensuring that the overall requirements and the organization's strategy are maintained throughout the entire planning process, the same way the voice of the customer is maintained throughout the entire product development process under ordinary use of the tool. It is a general approach to analyzing relationships between ends and means to achieve these, and is well suited also for improvement planning.

This is best illustrated by a practical example. In the following, QFD is used to develop the performance requirements set for the process of production planning. The resulting house of quality is shown in Figure 5.15, which has been developed using the software QFD Designer (Rolstadås, 1995). When it comes to QFD computer programs, there are a number of companies who offer such software. The author has been using QFD Designer, but positive reviews have been given of both QFD Capture and QFD Scope. Both of these can be tested by downloading free sample programs from the Internet.

First, the external performance requirements or performance demands the chosen strategy poses for this process are defined in WHAT. In the WHY field, some sort of benchmarking has been performed by collecting data from the main customers and suppliers through the use of a questionnaire. By plotting the performance of the competitors along with an organization's own performance, this field portrays current gap status.

In HOW, more operational means to achieving the ends in WHAT have been defined, typically grouped into subsets. Next, an analysis has been undertaken to determine relations between ends and means, as indicated in the relational matrix. As can be seen from the chart, two of the WHAT elements have not been assigned any relation symbols to any of the elements of HOW. This means that production planning, the process being analyzed, does not have any impact on these two performance requirements. They must thus be covered by other efforts.

In the next field, goals for the means have been defined—for example, time-to-market of six months for launching new products. These goals must be operational and measurable to enable follow-up. The chart shows, however, that it has not been possible to define good and relevant goals for all the means elements of HOW. By comparing the goals with other organizations, input for displaying performance gaps and contributing to adjustments of these goals is achieved.

The roof of the house of quality shows the relations between different means—for example, that a more efficient production and a reduction of defect rates both have a positive effect on lead times. On the other hand, there is a conflict between resource utilization and both flexibility and lead time. This information is very important when planning specific improvement efforts, as it enables avoiding two or more projects that work against each other.

As was described earlier, the absolute importance of each of the elements in HOW is calculated and placed in the line below the goals. The distribution in percentages is also calculated to illustrate the relative importance of each HOW element in relation to the others. Because it is obvious that some of these elements are easier to improve than others, the chart also offers the opportunity to appoint a factor expressing organizational obstacles against implementation. In this field of the chart, a factor of 3 indicates an

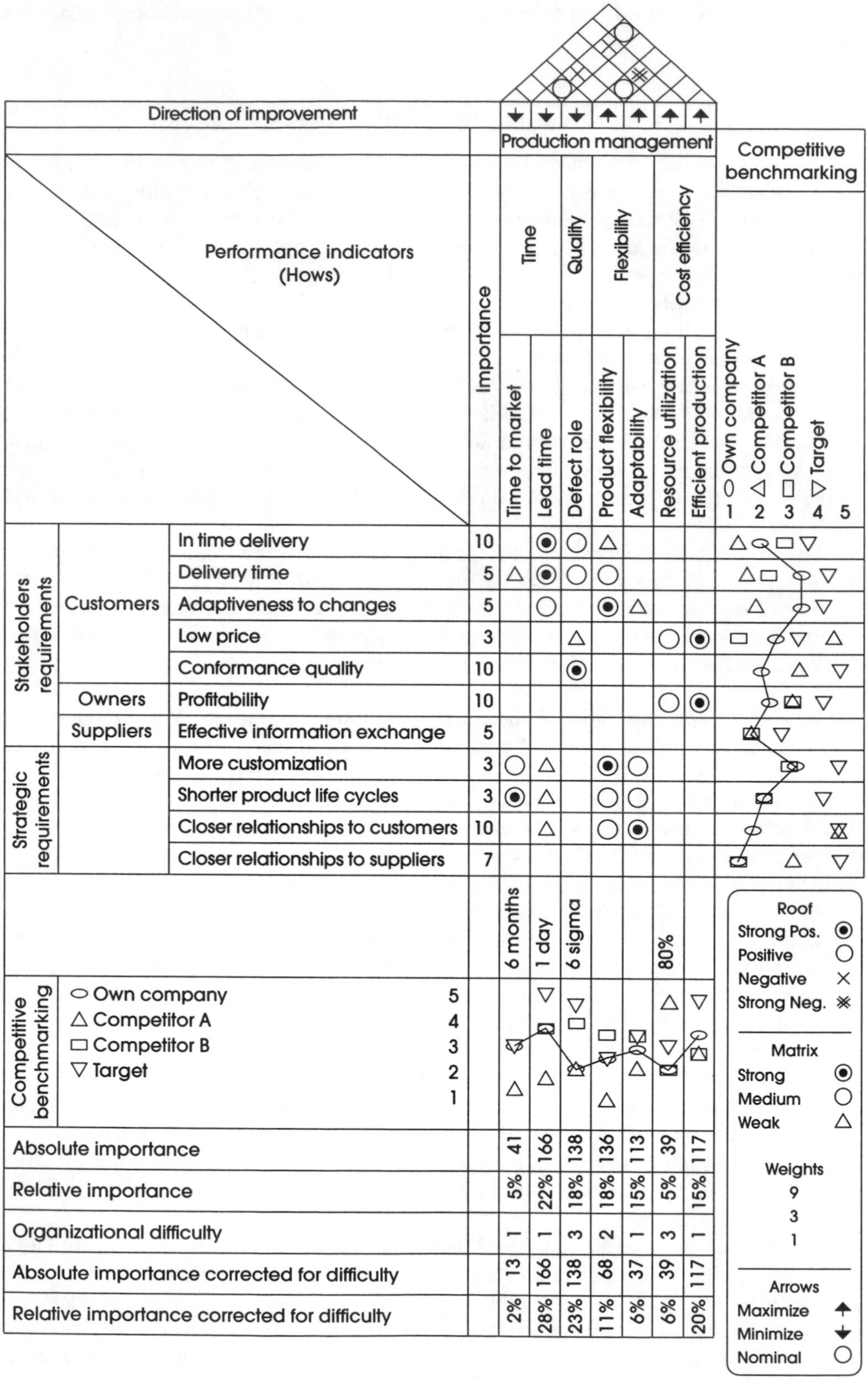

		Performance indicators (Hows)	Importance	Time Time to market	Lead time	Quality Defect role	Flexibility Product flexibility	Adaptability	Resource utilization	Cost efficiency Efficient production	Competitive benchmarking ○ Own company △ Competitor A □ Competitor B ▽ Target 1 2 3 4 5
Stakeholders requirements	Customers	In time delivery	10	◉	○	△					△ ○ □ ▽
		Delivery time	5	△	◉	○	○				△ □ ○ ▽
		Adaptiveness to changes	5	○		◉	△				△ ○ ▽
		Low price	3		△			○	◉		□ ○ ▽ △
		Conformance quality	10		◉						○ △ ▽
	Owners	Profitability	10					○	◉		○ □ △ ▽
	Suppliers	Effective information exchange	5								□△ ▽
Strategic requirements		More customization	3	○	△	◉	○				□○ ▽
		Shorter product life cycles	3	◉	△		○	○			□○ ▽
		Closer relationships to customers	10		△		○	◉			□△
		Closer relationships to suppliers	7								□△ △ ▽

				6 months	1 day	6 sigma				80%	Roof Strong Pos. ◉ Positive ○ Negative × Strong Neg. ※
Competitive benchmarking	○ Own company		5		▽	▽			△	▽	
	△ Competitor A		4		□△	□	□	□△	▽	○○	Matrix Strong ◉ Medium ○ Weak △
	□ Competitor B		3	▽		□△		□△	□△	□△	
	▽ Target		2		△						Weights 9 3 1
			1	△	△	△		△			
Absolute importance				41	166	138	136	113	39	117	
Relative importance				5%	22%	18%	18%	15%	5%	15%	
Organizational difficulty				1	1	3	2	1	3	1	Arrows Maximize ▲ Minimize ▼ Nominal ○
Absolute importance corrected for difficulty				13	166	138	68	37	39	117	
Relative importance corrected for difficulty				2%	28%	23%	11%	6%	6%	20%	

Direction of improvement: ▼ ▼ ▼ ▲ ▲ ▲ ▲

Production management

Figure 5.15. Example of a house of quality for production planning.

element that is difficult to implement, while 1 is considered quite straightforward. By including this factor in the calculations, the two last rows express absolute and relative importance adjusted for organizational difficulty.

The resulting chart shows that improving lead times, more efficient production, and defect rates are the key elements to satisfying the external and strategic performance requirements. From the roof of the chart, we also remember that these three elements probably to some extent will reinforce the effects from each other.

This example should help demonstrate that QFD is a powerful tool for deriving and designing improvement strategies that can contribute to a complex set of performance requirements. It helps visualize potential conflicts between different improvement approaches and forces the organization to develop a coherent set of tactics.

The result of the use of the different tools presented in this chapter will be a prioritization of what business processes or areas of the organization that should be improved. The next chapters focus on specific tools for problem analysis and improvement of single processes.

REFERENCES

Akao, Yoji, ed. *Quality Function Deployment: Integrating Customer Requirements Into Product Design*. Productivity Press, Cambridge, Massachusetts, USA, 1990.

Andersen, Bjørn, and Per-Gaute Pettersen, *The Benchmarking Handbook: Step-by-Step Instructions*. Chapman & Hall, London, England, 1996.

Rolstadås, Asbjørn, ed. *Performance Management: A Business Process Benchmarking Approach*. Chapman & Hall, London, England, 1995.

CHAPTER 6

Improvement Tools

In this chapter, a brief presentation is given of the toolbox available for improvement efforts. The different tools are classified according to different criteria and very briefly described. A far more detailed treatment of each single tool is given in the following chapters. Some of the tools have been collected from different sources, the most important ones being Aune (1993), Mizuno (1988), Rolstadås (1995), Swanson (1995), Harrington (1991), Lawlor (1985), and Eastman Kodak Company (1990).

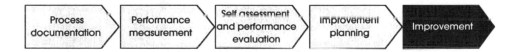

6.1 Classification of Improvement Tools

As will become apparent, there are many different tools and techniques in this improvement toolbox. Viewed as a complete set, there are significant differences among many of these. To make the presentation of them as clear as possible, it has been attempted to classify the tools. This can be done according to a number of criteria, including:

- The extent of change resulting from using the tools
- Requirements for time and resources when using the tools
- Improvement focus or main purpose of the tools
- Source for improvement impulses

The world, fortunately, is not sufficiently square that all the tools can be singularly defined for each criterion and thus placed in the right category. The classification has been carried out based on the most prominent features of the tools and in complete confidence that exceptions exist.

6.1.1 The Main Purpose of the Tools

Under this heading, an attempt has been made at grouping the tools according to what their main purpose is—for example, problem identification or purely improvement. Some tools can contribute to more than one objective, but as was mentioned, the classification is based on the most visible characteristic. Within the phase of improvement in the overall improvement model, as depicted in Figure 2.2, some further stages with different detailed content can be defined, as shown in Figure 6.1. The presentation of the tools throughout the book follows this order of the stages.

Some tools have already been presented that can assist the task of prioritizing the improvement effort through analyzing which business processes or areas of the organization are in need of improvement. These are:

- Self assessment, to form an overall impression of the organization's performance level.

- Trend analysis, to evaluate the development of the organization's performance level in the aftermath of a self assessment.

- Spider chart, to view the organization's own performance level in light of that of organizations with which it is logically compared.

- Performance matrix, where the objective is to analyze the different business processes' need for improvement based on their importance and current performance level.

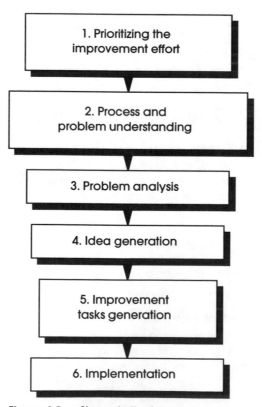

Figure 6.1.   Stages in the improvement work.

- Criteria testing, which is a numerical tool for analyzing which business processes have the highest impact on the critical success factors of the organization.

- QFD, which in this context is used for performing a coherent planning of the organization's improvement activity by considering both external requirements and demands posed by the strategy.

After deciding which process should be improved, the next logical step is to document and understand the process, both on a higher level and with regard to more detailed problems within the process. Tools for this purpose are:

- Relationship mapping, which has been treated earlier.

- Flowchart, which originally is one of the seven tools for problem-solving. It has also been described in much detail in the chapter dealing with process documentation, chapter 3, and will not be revisited.

- Critical incident, which is a technique for identifying problems within an area or process.

- Check sheet, another one of the seven tools for problem-solving, which is used for collecting data about a process or problem area.

- Pareto chart, another one of the seven, to sort problems or causes according to importance.

Another important stage in the improvement work is problem analysis. Some tools in this class are:

- Cause-and-effect chart, further one of the seven problem-solving tools, whose purpose is to identify causes to a problem.

- Root cause analysis, also termed why-why chart.

- Scatter chart, another one of the seven, used to see connections between phenomena.

- Histogram, the fifth of the seven, to sort data about a process in a clear manner.

- Relations diagram, one of the seven tools for quality management, whose objective is to help find links between effects and probable causes for these.

- Matrix diagram, to graphically portray data and see connections and relations.

Further on, there are several tools for idea generation:

- Brainstorming, the most basic of these techniques, where the idea is to create as many ideas as possible.

- Brainwriting/Crawford slip method, which is close to a written version of brainstorming.

- Nominal group technique, which is a more formalized way of generating ideas.

- Affinity chart, to organize thoughts or ideas.

Pure improvement tools—that is, whose main purpose is to achieve improvements—include:

- Streamlining, which is a common term for several principles for simplifying business processes, eliminating waste, and increasing the efficiency.

- Idealizing, whose purpose is to find the ideal process when disregarding practical limitations.

- Quality function deployment, QFD, potentially combined with a system diagram, in this context to design products or processes based on customer requirements.

- Work unit analysis, to analyze the customer/supplier relationship between segments of a business process to improve the interfaces between them.

- Statistical process control and the use of the last of the seven tools for problem-solving, control chart.

- Business process reengineering, one of the "hotter" tools lately.

- Benchmarking, which seeks to create improvements through learning from other organizations.

A last group contains tools or techniques aimed at planning the implementation of improvement and setting targets for these:

- Tree diagram, one of the seven tools for quality management, used for planning a project—for example, an improvement implementation.

- Process decision program chart, another of these seven tools, used to prevent undesirable events from occurring.

- AΔT analysis, used to set ambitious targets for the improvement activity.

Force field analysis, whose purpose is to identify forces working for and against an implementation of improvements.

6.1.2 Extent of Change

By *extent of change* is meant how dramatic changes in the process steps, organization, and so on, can be expected when using a tool. While some tools typically will lead to only minor adjustments, others can cause radically changed processes. At the end of the scale containing tools that generally cause the least changes, we find:

- The two groups of seven tools each—that is, the seven tools for problem-solving and the seven tools for quality management

- Tools for idea generation

- Critical incident

- Statistical process control

Somewhat larger changes can be expected when using the following tools:

- Streamlining

- Work unit analysis

- Quality function deployment

At the other end of the scale—that is, tools that generally lead to major changes—the following are found:

- Idealizing

- Business process reengineering

- Benchmarking, as all three often cause larger redesigns in processes

6.1.3 Time and Resource Requirements

This obviously means how much time and how much of other resources—for example, direct expenses—the organization should anticipate setting aside for using a tool. Among those requiring the least resources are:

- The seven traditional and the seven new tools

- Critical incident

- Tools for idea generation

- Idealizing

In the middle, the following techniques reside:

- Work unit analysis

- Streamlining

- Statistical process control

- Quality function deployment

As for extent of change, the following two are also among those that require the most resources:

- Business process reengineering

- Benchmarking

6.1.4 Source for Improvement Impulses

When it comes to this last criterion for classification, the subject is from where the tool collects impulses and ideas for improvement. Classifying according to this criterion is really very simple, as all the tools, except for benchmarking, advocate internal generation of improvement ideas. In this respect, benchmarking is quite different from the others, as the entire concept of benchmarking is based on obtaining impulses from the outside.

6.2   Organizational Methods

In addition to the more specific tools and techniques summarized above, a few methods or principles related to organizational aspects that can be useful for improvement will also be presented. These are:

- Cross-functional teams

- Problem-solving teams

- Quality circles

In the following chapters, each of these tools and techniques is described in detail, and in the order of the classification based on the *purpose* of the tools.

REFERENCES

Aune, Asbjørn. *Kvalitetsstyrte bedrifter* (the title translates to *Quality-Managed Companies*). Ad Notam, Oslo, Norway, 1993.

Eastman Kodak Company. *Quality Leadership Process Guidebook*. Eastman Kodak Company, Rochester, New York, USA, 1990.

Harrington, H. James. *Business Process Improvement: The Breakthrough Strategy for Total Quality, Productivity, and Competitiveness*. McGraw-Hill, New York, USA, 1991.

Lawlor, Alan. *Productivity Improvement Manual*. Gower Publishing, Aldershot, England, 1985.

Mizuno, Shigeru, ed. *Management for Quality Improvement: The 7 New QC Tools*. Productivity Press, Cambridge, Massachusetts, USA, 1988.

Rolstadås, Asbjørn, ed. *Performance Management: A Business Process Benchmarking Approach*. Chapman & Hall, London, England.

Straker, David. *A Toolbook for Quality Improvement and Problem Solving*. Prentice-Hall, London, England, 1995.

Swanson, Roger C. *The Quality Improvement Handbook: Team Guide to Tools and Techniques*. Kogan Page, London, England, 1995.

CHAPTER 7

Tools for Problem Understanding

In the improvement planning, it will usually be decided which business process or area of the organization it is wise to improve. This indication is often quite coarse—for example, in the shape of a decision to improve the product development process. Within this decision, there is a need to perform a more detailed analysis of the process, not in the least to define what specific problem we want to solve. This is also closely related to the need for a clearer understanding of how the process is carried out today. Four central tools in this group are:

- Flowchart, which is primarily suited for process documentation. The flowchart has been thoroughly described earlier, and it is recommended that the pure process documentation task is carried out at an earlier stage in the improvement process. Nevertheless, the flowchart is a tool that can also be used for producing a more detailed description of the process containing more information than the overall description.

- Critical incident

- Check sheet

- Pareto chart

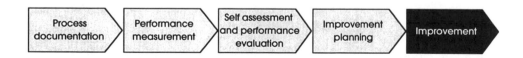

7.1 Critical Incident

Critical incident is a technique designed to assist in the identification of a process, subprocess, or a problem area that should be improved (Lawlor, 1985). It is a quite open and frank way of seeking information about organizational problems, as a prerequisite is that the participants are completely free to express their views. In this respect, it is important that management displays the right attitudes to avoid censorship or withholding of information in fear of consequences from being too honest.

The technique works as follows:

1. First, the participants for the analysis are selected. If the objective is to decide on the overall process to be improved, it is natural to include representatives from a number of areas within the organization. If the purpose is to more precisely define the focus within an already selected business process, people actively involved in this process are chosen.

2. Next, the group of participants is asked to answer questions like:

   • Which incident last week was most difficult to handle?

   • Which episode created the biggest problems in terms of maintaining customer satisfaction?

   • Which incident cost the most in terms of extra resources or direct expenditures?

The purpose is to focus on the so-called critical incidents that in one way or another created problems for the employees, the organization, or other stakeholders. The period covered by the questions can range from a few days to several months. It is, however, not favorable if the period is too long, as it might be difficult to determine the most critical incident simply because many incidents can qualify as candidates given a sufficient length of time.

3. The collected answers are sorted and analyzed based on the number of times the different incidents have been mentioned. A graphical representation format might very well be used for this purpose. The incidents occurring most often—such as the critical ones—will be obvious candidates for prevention of recurrence. It should also be pointed out that it is not the incident itself that must be attacked, but the causes for it. Tools to identify the cause, not the symptom, are treated in chapter 8.

A large corporation with a staff of 15 switchboard operators started a project to improve the customer service when answering phones. It was difficult to decide in which end of this area to start, so it was decided to try the technique of critical incident.

All the operators were asked to describe the most embarrassing situations they had experienced the last month. The resulting events were sorted by frequency and presented in a chart as shown in Figure 7.1. As the diagram shows, the most critical incidents were not reaching the person who should handle a call, or not knowing who should handle it. This resulted in efforts focused around designing a system to keep track of the individual employee and drawing up clearer rules for who should handle what requests.

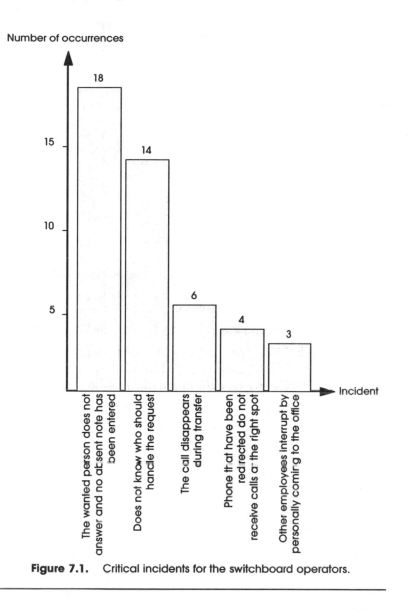

Figure 7.1. Critical incidents for the switchboard operators.

7.2 Check Sheet

A *check sheet* is a table or form used for registering data as they are collected (Rolstadås, 1995). One of the main applications is registering how often different problems or incidents occur. This provides important information about problem areas or probable causes for errors, and thus provides a good foundation for deciding where to concentrate during improvement.

The approach is normally as follows:

1. Agreement is reached about what events are to be recorded. These must be clearly defined to avoid doubt whether an event truly occurred. It is usually also smart to include a category of "others" to capture incidents that are not easy to otherwise categorize.

Problem	Week 1	Week 2	Week 3	Total number of occur- rences per problem
A	𝑇𝐻𝐿 ///	𝑇𝐻𝐿 //	𝑇𝐻𝐿 𝑇𝐻𝐿 //	27
B	//	/	/	4
C	/	𝑇𝐻𝐿 𝑇𝐻𝐿 //	𝑇𝐻𝐿 𝑇𝐻𝐿	23
D	𝑇𝐻𝐿 𝑇𝐻𝐿 𝑇𝐻𝐿 //	𝑇𝐻𝐿 𝑇𝐻𝐿 𝑇𝐻𝐿 𝑇𝐻𝐿 ///	𝑇𝐻𝐿 𝑇𝐻𝐿 ///	53
E	//	////	///	9
F		/	/	2
G			//	2
H	𝑇𝐻𝐿 /	𝑇𝐻𝐿 //	/	14
Total number of problems per week	36	55	43	134

Figure 7.2.   Example of a check sheet.

2. Define the period for data recording and a suitable division into intervals.

3. Design the check sheet to be used during recording. An example is shown in Figure 7.2, where space is allocated for recording each event and summarizing both within the intervals and for the entire recording period.

4. Perform data collection during the agreed period. In advance, it is necessary to make sure that everyone taking part in the data collection has a common understanding of the task, so as to achieve consistency in the data material.

5. When data collection is completed, the material is analyzed to identify events displaying a high number of occurrences. These will contribute to the prioritization of what specific areas within the chosen business process should be emphasized in the ensuing improvement work. A suitable visual aid for this analysis is a Pareto chart, which is presented on page 70 (see Figure 7.4).

The danger of overlooking one or more categories of problems should also be mentioned. If we are exclusively looking for events of the type defined in the check sheet, other problems might occur, but fail to be recorded as the attention is directed only toward the expected problems. This is partly supposed to be countered by the inclusion of an "others" category, but this issue should still be kept in mind. For easy construction of check sheets and also generation of Pareto charts based on the collected data, the PC program, The Memory Jogger Software, can be used.

A medium-sized company in the electrical installation industry annually submits a large number of bids for jobs for both private and industrial customers. The company was not satisfied with the portion of bids that resulted in jobs, and therefore wanted to follow up and improve the process of generating bids.

To obtain an overview of the major causes why the company was not assigned more jobs, the check sheet shown in Figure 7.3 was designed. Each time a bid was rejected by the potential customer or the bid of a competitor was preferred, the customer was asked to explain the reasons. The responses were entered into the check sheet during a period of three months.

Cause of lost bid	January	February	March	Total number of occurrences per cause
Too high price	//	///	//	7
Poor quality	//	/	/	4
Low flexibility	𝈫𝈫 𝈫𝈫 𝈫𝈫	𝈫𝈫 𝈫𝈫 //	𝈫𝈫 𝈫𝈫 ///	40
Poor impression during inspection	///	//	///	8
Low technical expertise	/	//	//	5
Total number of causes per month	23	20	21	64

Figure 7.3.   Check sheet for recording the causes for lost bids.

As the sheet indicated, price was not the dominating reason for rejection, contrary to what the company had believed. The problem was rather very often a lack of flexibility with regard to when the job could be carried out. The result was that a new system for monitoring the availability of the service workers was designed. In addition, it was made clear in every single bid that the work could be started on very short notice and very well be carried out in several separate periods, all at once, during evenings, whenever. In the long run, this resulted in a radical increase in the portion of won bids, and at substantially better prices.

7.3   Pareto Chart

The Pareto chart is based on the so-called Pareto principle, formulated by the Italian mathematician Vilfredo Pareto during the 1800s (Rolstadås, 1995). He was concerned with the distribution of the riches in society, and claimed that 20 percent of the population owned 80 percent of the wealth. Translated to the modern quality terminology, the Pareto principle states that most of the effects, often around 80 percent, are caused by a small number of causes, often only 20 percent. For example, usually 80 percent of the problems related to purchased material are caused by 20 percent of the suppliers. Even more importantly, 80 percent of all costs connected to poor quality or generally low performance is caused by 20 percent of all possible causes. A healthy approach is therefore to start the improvement work by attacking these 20 percent, which are often labeled "the vital few." This does not imply that the remaining 80 percent should be ignored; "these important many" should in due time also be addressed. The Pareto principle only says something about the order in which the problems should be attacked.

The Pareto chart itself is a tool used to display graphically this skewed distribution, the so-called 80–20 rule. The chart shows the causes to a problem sorted by the degree of seriousness, expressed as frequency of occurrence, costs, performance level, and so on. The causes are sorted by placing the most severe ones on the left side of the chart, rendering it quite easy to identify the vital few. To enable portraying further information in the chart, it is common practice to also include a curve showing cumulative importance. This is depicted in Figure 7.4.

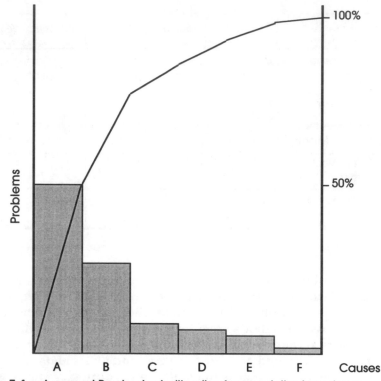

Figure 7.4. A general Pareto chart with a line for cumulative importance.

When using a Pareto chart, the most common steps are to:

1. Define the main problem and the different potential causes for it. According to the improvement process recommended in this book, the main processes desired to be improved will already have been selected and the purpose of the Pareto chart is thus to identify the main causes for a low performance level.

2. Decide which quantitative measure to use when comparing the possible causes. As has been mentioned, this measure might be how often the different problems occur or consequences of them in terms of costing money or other conditions.

3. Define the time interval during which data will be collected and carry out the data collection. Often, this last task will already have been performed by the use of a check sheet, as described in the preceding section.

4. Place the causes from left to right along the horizontal axis in descending relative importance. Draw rectangles of heights that represent this importance.

5. Mark the data value itself on the left vertical axis and the percentage value on the right, and draw the curve for cumulative importance along the top edge of the rectangles.

A quick inspection of the chart can now answer questions like, "What are the two to three main causes for the low performance level of this process?" or, "How large a portion of the costs can be attributed to the most vital causes?" This information can be used for actively directing the improvement efforts toward areas that are likely to produce the best effects.

Pareto charts can easily be constructed using standard spreadsheet software. However, there is specialized software available for this type of charting. Two such programs are StatGraphics Plus and SAS/QC software, which also allows the user to generate statistical process control charts. Furthermore, The Memory Jogger software contains capabilities for several typical quality improvement tools.

The installation company in the example about check sheets also drew a Pareto chart displaying the collected data. Instead of how often different reasons were given for why the company's bid did not win, the value of the lost job was assigned to the vertical axis. The resulting chart can be seen in Figure 7.5.

The chart confirmed that the low flexibility expressed to the customers regarding how quickly and at what time of day the work could be done not only was the most frequent reason for failures to win bids, but also caused

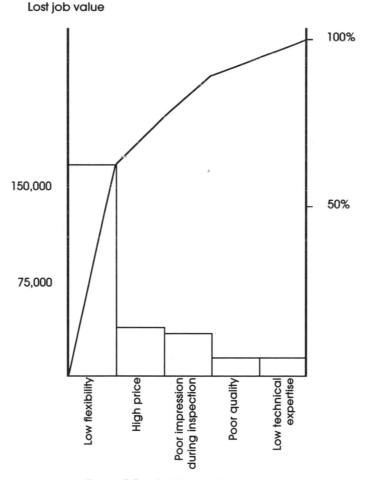

Figure 7.5. Pareto chart for lost job value.

the biggest losses in terms of lost job value. It was, in other words, right to aim for a new system for planning the work in the company.

REFERENCES

Lawlor, Alan. *Productivity Improvement Manual.* Gower Publishing, Aldershot, England, 1985.

Rolstadås, Asbjørn, ed. *Performance Management: A Business Process Benchmarking Approach.* Chapman & Hall, London, England, 1995.

CHAPTER 8

Tools for Problem Analysis

The preceding chapter dealt with tools for problem understanding, tools that are suitable for defining the problem and limiting the focus of the improvement effort—for example, by selecting specific segments of a business process. This scope definition can be defined to mark the end of the improvement planning, or at least the transition from improvement planning to the improvement stage itself. After having been through this problem understanding stage, the next step is to work on identifying specific causes for problems and solutions to these. By the way, the line between these stages is not very clearly defined; some of the tools described in the preceding chapter can also be used for problem analysis. The tools treated here are:

- Cause-and-effect chart
- Root cause analysis
- Scatter chart
- Histogram
- Relations diagram
- Matrix diagram

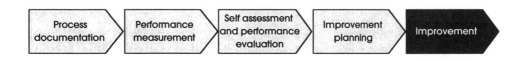

8.1   Cause-and-Effect Chart

This is one of the classical and most widely used tools in quality management, and not without reason. Many view the tool as being somewhat old-fashioned and sturdy in a rather boring sense, but it is truly a useful tool with many powers. The main purpose is, as the name implies, to identify possible causes for an effect (Rolstadås, 1995). The effect being analyzed can be both an experienced problem or a future hoped-for state. This way, the chart can be used both for finding causes for problems and planning how to reach a state where they no longer occur.

The chart has so far been described as if it were one singular chart, but the fact is that there are at least two types of cause-and-effect charts:

- Fishbone chart

- Process chart

8.1.1 Fishbone Chart

This is the traditional way of constructing such charts, where the main product is a chart whose shape resembles a fishbone. The main principles for such a chart are shown in Figure 8.1. There are, however, two ways of creating the chart:

- Dispersion analysis, where the effect being analyzed is drawn on the right side of the chart, at the end of a large arrow. Main groups of probable causes are drawn as branches to the arrow. For each branch, all possible causes are identified.

- Cause enumeration, where all probable causes are simply brainstormed and listed in the order they are generated. When this has been done, the causes are grouped into main groups and drawn in the fishbone chart. The end product is the same regardless of the approach.

The main steps for producing a fishbone chart using dispersion analysis, which is the more common approach, are:

1. The chart can naturally be used by individuals, but usually does give better results when created in a group. The first step is therefore to assemble a suitable group possessing the necessary knowledge about the area to be analyzed.

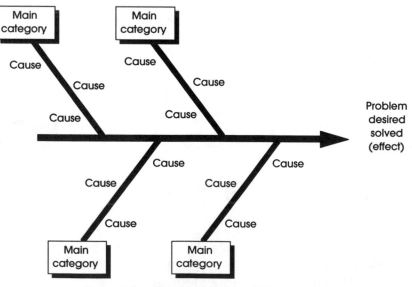

Figure 8.1.   The structure for a fishbone chart.

2. Describe clearly the effect for which causes are sought. This effect is often a low performance level for one of the business processes of the organization.

3. Using a white board or some other large medium, draw the effect at the end of a large arrow. The point is to set aside enough space for the generated causes, not symmetry and nice drawing effects.

4. Identify the main categories of possible causes for the effect and place these at branches emanating from the large arrow. For physical processes, some common main categories are:

- People

- Machines and equipment

- Materials

- Methods

- Measures

- Environment—that is, culture, organizational structure, physical environment, and so on.

Similarly, for service processes, the traditional categories are:

- People

- Processes

- Frame conditions

- Work environment

5. Brainstorm all possible causes and place these in the suitable area of the chart. Emphasize brief and succinct descriptions. Proceed through the chart one main category at the time, but also include surfacing suggestions that belong to categories other than the one currently being treated. Causes that belong to more than one category are placed in all relevant positions. It is often required to redraw the chart after the first version has been completed.

6. Analyze the identified causes to determine the most important ones, the ones that should be addressed further. Remember that the purpose is always to cure the problem, not the symptoms!

Even though the process of constructing the chart is equally important as the chart itself, one can use software for constructing the cause-and-effect chart. Three programs with the capabilities for this are allClear, AutoCad, and CADKEY.

8.1.2 Process Chart

This variant of the chart is more directly aimed at improvement of business processes. The main steps in the process to be improved are drawn. For each step of the process believed to create problems or contribute to a low overall performance level, a fishbone chart is constructed that deals with all potential causes why this step performs less than expected. For each of these individual fishbone charts, the process is the same as outlined above for constructing such a chart.

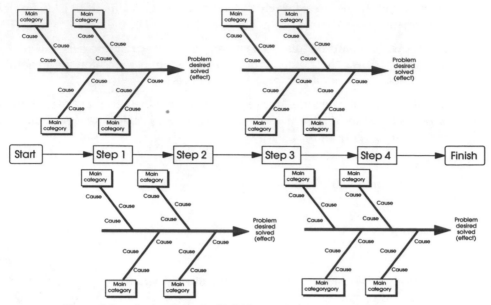

Figure 8.2.   Process chart with fishbone charts for each process step.

After having designed individual charts for each problem step of the process, a collective analysis is undertaken to identify the causes seemingly being of highest importance. For these, solutions are sought that can reduce the negative effects on the overall performance level of the process. The resulting chart might look like the one shown in Figure 8.2.

A pump manufacturer experienced frequent defects in a series of pumps delivered to a customer. Closer inspection revealed that most of the defects stemmed from inaccurate dimensions of two shafts used in the pumps. A group consisting of designers, the manufacturing manager, the shaft department manager, and several operators was established. The objective was to find and eliminate the causes for the problems. The design of the fishbone chart in Figure 8.3 gave some clues as to where the problems might be found.

Most importantly, it became evident that the physical environment in which the shafts were manufactured was rather unsuitable for the process, as a low temperature in the shop combined with the wrong coolant resulted in most of the dimension errors.

8.2   Root Cause Analysis

This technique is also known as the "why-why chart" and "five whys." As these names imply, the purpose is to find the true root cause of a problem (Andersen and Pettersen, 1996). The technique can very well be used in connection with a cause-and-effect chart, then to analyze each identified cause to ensure that it really is the root cause of the problem, not only a symptom of another and more deeply rooted cause. This can in

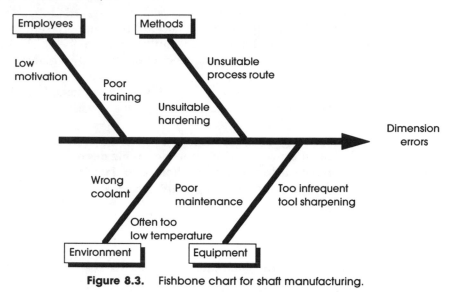

Figure 8.3.   Fishbone chart for shaft manufacturing.

fact be compared with peeling an onion, where each layer is removed to reveal another one, until the center of the onion is reached.

The procedure for conducting a root cause analysis is:

1. Determine the starting point, either a problem or a high-level cause that should be further analyzed.

2. Use brainstorming to find causes at the level below the starting point.

3. For each identified cause, pose the question, "Why is this a cause for the original problem?"

4. For each new answer to the question, ask the question again and again until no new answers result. This will probably be one of the root causes for the problem. As a rule of thumb, this often requires five rounds of the question "Why?"

If the question is twisted slightly to asking "how" instead of asking "why," the technique can be used to find root means for reaching a desired state or effect. Practically, the analysis can be conducted in different ways. A graphically visible way of keeping track of the different levels of causes is listing them below one another, as shown in Figure 8.4. In this example, it has been attempted to find means for reducing the amount of work-in-progress in a manufacturing company. The result of the analysis was that the key word to reducing the work-in-progress is developing good

Low level of Work-in-Progress	
Why?	Maintain no stock of finished goods
Why?	Short manufacturing time
Why?	Run small batch sizes
Why?	Frequent and swift deliveries from the suppliers
Why?	Extremely good relationships to the suppliers

Figure 8.4.   List representation of five whys.

relationships with the suppliers. If this analysis had not been undertaken, the company might be led to believe that the answer was simply to remove the finished goods inventory, which could have had serious consequences. Alternatively, a diagram might be used to portray an entire network of causes at different levels, as shown in the example below. Furthermore, for those preferring to work with computers, Reason Point of Occurrence is a program that can be used for root cause analysis.

A video rental chain had experienced an ever-increasing degree of customer dissatisfaction when measuring customer satisfaction data. A simple questionnaire revealed that the four most important causes were:

- **Long check-out times**

- **Poor selection of titles**

- **Impolite and unfriendly personnel**

- **Unfavorable store location and layout**

Through a root cause analysis, the chart in Figure 8.5 was constructed. Most of the problems could thus be attributed to low wages and low management expertise.

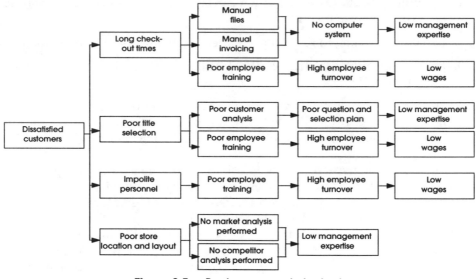

Figure 8.5.   Root cause analysis chart.

8.3   Scatter Chart

A scatter chart can be used to show the relationship between two variables (Rolstadås, 1995). The variables can be process characteristics, performance measures, or other conditions, and are usually measured at specified time intervals. When one of the factors increases, the other can either also increase, decrease, or display only random variation. If the two variables seem to change in synchronization, it might mean that they are related and impact each other. For example, we could find that the number of defects increases in proportion with the amount of overtime used. However, keep in mind that even if there is some degree of synchronized variation between variables, it does not say for certain that there is a cause-and-effect relationship between them. It may very well be a third variable that is causing the effects. This can be illustrated by the fact that a scatter chart was once constructed that showed an obvious correlation between the Dow Jones index and the water level of Lake Superior in the years between 1925 and 1965.

The degree of relationship between the variables being examined can range from highly positive to highly negative correlation. Between these two extremes, there are weaker degrees of both positive and negative correlation, as well as no correlation. Figure 8.6 shows some examples of different scatter charts for different degrees of correlation.

When using a scatter chart, the following steps are usually conducted:

1. Select the two variables, one independent and one dependent, to be examined.

2. For each value of the independent variable, the corresponding value of the dependent value is measured. These two values form a data pair to be plotted in the chart. Typically, there should be at least 30, but preferably more than 100, data pairs to produce a meaningful chart.

3. Draw the chart itself placing the independent variable—that is, the expected cause variable—on the x axis, and the dependent, expected effect variable, on the y axis.

4. Plot the collected data pairs on the chart and analyze it. If the chart shows no correlation, the data pairs can be drawn in a logarithmic chart. Such a chart can reveal connections that are not visible in a chart with ordinary axes.

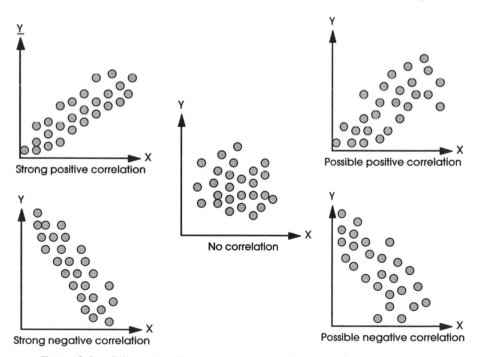

Figure 8.6. Different scatter charts showing different degrees of correlation.

Producing a scatter chart by hand, at least with some amount of data, can be tedious work. A spreadsheet software does that job much easier. One can also buy programs suited for specialized purposes like constructing different quality tool charts—for example, The Memory Jogger Software, which can generate scatter charts. Remember, if a chart indicates a relationship, the variables should be further analyzed to confirm this. In the same way, a chart showing no relationship should not automatically lead to a conclusion that no relationship exists.

As part of the efforts to create an improved state of readiness for performing rush jobs, the electric installation company we looked at earlier wanted to examine the relationship between the amount of jobs—and thus the need for ready servicemen—and the weather type. Through a quarter of a year, the company counted every week the number of days with thunder or lightning, as well as the number of jobs. The scatter chart that was designed (see Figure 8.7) displayed a clear correlation between bad weather and the amount of jobs. As a response, the company started considering the weather forecasts when planning capacity and the possibility for reserve capacity.

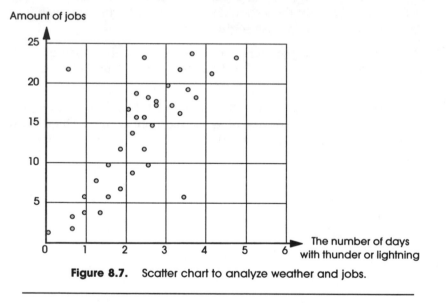

Figure 8.7.   Scatter chart to analyze weather and jobs.

8.4   Histogram

A histogram, or a bar chart as it is also called, is used to display the distribution and variation for a measure of some sort (Rolstadås, 1995). The measure can be an infinite number of different aspects—for example, length, diameter, duration, costs, and so on. The same information can also be presented in a table, but presented in such a manner, it can be difficult to spot important patterns in the data material. The graphic presentation format usually renders it easier to see relationships. Unlike the Pareto chart, which is really a variant of a histogram that displays the frequency of occurrence for a phenomenon, intervals of data are usually portrayed in a histogram.

9.9	9.9	10.4	9.8	10.1	10.2	9.8	10.3	9.7	9.7
9.8	9.3	10.2	9.3	9.2	9.8	9.8	10.1	9.8	9.8
9.7	9.8	10.2	9.8	10.2	10.0	9.7	9.5	9.6	9.5
10.2	9.4	10.1	10.1	9.6	9.7	10.0	10.0	9.3	9.5
9.9	10.1	9.6	9.7	9.6	9.5	9.7	9.7	10.0	9.7
9.3	10.7	9.8	9.8	9.8	9.9	9.6	9.7	9.7	9.9
9.0	10.2	9.3	10.3	9.9	9.9	10.1	10.7	10.7	9.6
10.0	9.5	9.2	9.9	10.0	10.1	10.0	9.8	9.4	9.3
9.5	9.7	9.7	9.7	9.8	10.2	10.4	9.6	9.9	
9.6	9.7	9.4	9.8	9.9	10.3	9.8	10.0	10.0	
10.3	9.4	10.6	9.4	9.8	9.8	9.5	10.7	10.1	
9.5	9.6	10.1	10.1	9.6	9.3	9.5	9.9	10.3	
9.9	9.5	9.7	10.1	10.0	10.0	9.6	9.4	9.9	

Table 8.1.   The data material for the example with the diameter of holes.

8.4.1 Constructing a Histogram

The construction of a histogram follows the steps outlined below. The procedure is illustrated using an example where the diameter of a hole has been measured for 125 work pieces. The data material is shown in Table 8.1.

1. Count the number of data points in the data material, which is labeled N. To produce a valid histogram, there should be at least 50 data points. In the example, $N = 125$.

2. Determine the numerical distance, R, between the largest and the smallest value in the data material. In the example, $R = 10.7 - 9.0 = 1.7$.

3. Depending on the number of data points, R is divided into a number of equally large classes, C. The number of classes can be found in Table 8.2. For $N = 125$ in the example, the number of classes should be between 7 and 12, thus deciding to use 10 classes—that is, $C = 10$.

The number of data points, N	The number of classes, C
Less than 50	5–7
50–100	6–10
100–250	7–12
More than 250	10–20

Table 8.2.   Determining the number of classes, C.

Class	Lower value	Upper value	Frequency	Total
1	9.0		/	1
2	9.2		7HL ////	9
3	9.4		7HL 7HL 7HL /	16
4	9.6		7HL 7HL 7HL 7HL 7HL //	27
5	9.8		7HL 7HL 7HL 7HL 7HL 7HL /	31
6	10.0		7HL 7HL 7HL 7HL ///	23
7	10.2		7HL 7HL //	12
8	10.4		//	2
9	10.6		////	4
10	10.8			0

Table 8.3. Check sheet for the example.

4. Determine the width of each class, labeled H. This is calculated using the following formula:

$$H = \frac{R}{C} = \frac{1.7}{10} = 0.17 \approx 0.2$$

As can be seen, the class width in the example is rounded off to 0.2, as the width should always have as many decimals as the data points themselves—that is, one decimal in this case.

5. Determine the lower and upper values for the individual classes. This is done by letting the smallest value in the data material become the lower value for the first class. The upper value for this class is then found by adding the class width to the lower value. In the example, the first class will span the range from 9.0 to 9.2. The next class starts at 9.2 and covers the values up to 9.4, and so on. Remember that the lower value always includes this value (that is, $\geq$ lower value), while the upper value only goes up to it (that is, < upper value). The value 9.2, in other words, belongs to the second class, not the first one.

6. To simplify the construction of the histogram, the data material is inserted into a check. For the example, the check sheet is shown Table 8.3.

7. Finally, the histogram is constructed based on the check sheet. The classes are marked along the horizontal axis and the frequency along the vertical. The distribution among the classes is indicated by bars. The resulting histogram for the example is shown in Figure 8.8. As can be seen, constructing a histogram can be somewhat complicated.

Let us imagine that this histogram was designed by a company manufacturing steel components supposed to have a hole of diameter between 7.5 and 10.5 millimeters. With the help of the diagram, the company can see that the process falls beyond the upper specification limit and will actually manufacture approximately 3 percent defects. This information can thus be used to adjust the process to avoid defects.

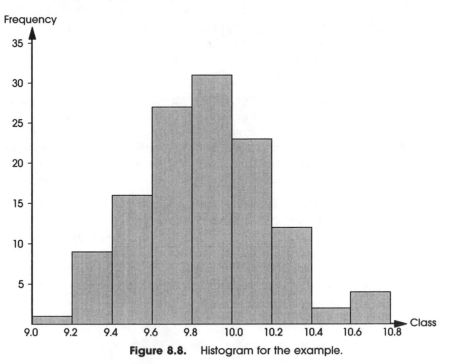

Figure 8.8. Histogram for the example.

8.4.2 Interpreting a Histogram

Using histograms this way is actually highly connected to statistical process control, which is treated in chapter 10. While a control chart in statistical process control contributes to a continuous monitoring of whether a process is under control, a histogram can reveal permanent deviations that do not appear in a control chart. Especially the shape of the histogram is the subject of close inspection and interpretation to reveal problems in the process.

Ideally, a histogram will produce an image of the variation in the data material while at the same time providing a sensible level of detail. If, however, too few classes have been defined, only a few bars will be the result, and these are not suited for revealing any patterns. Correspondingly, too many classes will hide the pattern since some will be empty, which results in an appearance resembling a comb.

Some particular patterns in the histogram indicate some typical problems in the process:

- A pattern with one obvious peak shows the mean value for the process. Depending on how much the process varies around this peak, the process is defined to be good or bad. A diagram like the one shown in Figure 8.9 is a process displaying a small variation width that lies centered within the specification limits. This is a good process. The diagram in Figure 8.10 shows a poorer process with a large variation width. If this cannot be reduced, the process will produce results outside the limits, which can be countered by conducting a 100 percent control.

- Furthermore, the location of the peak in diagrams with only one peak decides whether the process is under control. As was mentioned, the process in Figure 8.9 is a good process displaying little variation and being well centered within the limits. In Figure 8.11, another process with little variation is shown, but this one is not centered. Adjusting this process will give a good process.

- When the histogram displays two clear peaks, as shown in Figure 8.12, this can be the result of different causes. Either the data points can stem from two different sources, which should be checked or the process' mean value has changed during the data collection interval.

- A cut-off pattern—that is, a histogram ending abruptly showing no signs of tapering off—is a sign of control or selection of the results. This is shown in Figure 8.13 and is often visible close to tolerance limits. In this case, a control has probably been conducted and parts falling outside the limits have been removed from the data material. In these cases, we must know how much the defect parts cost. The process should be improved to avoid the defects.

- The previously mentioned comb-resembling pattern is an indication that too many classes have been defined. However, such a pattern can also be a result of problems with the measurement equipment. If the measurement equipment is unable to register points in the individual classes or with the accuracy required to use so many classes, such an appearance will be the result. In such a case, the measurement approach should be reevaluated.

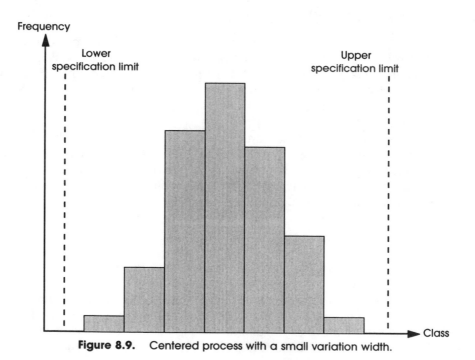

Figure 8.9.   Centered process with a small variation width.

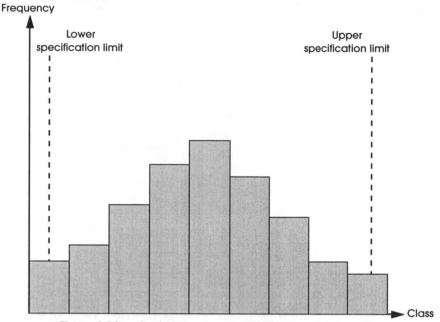

Figure 8.10.   Centered process with a large variation width.

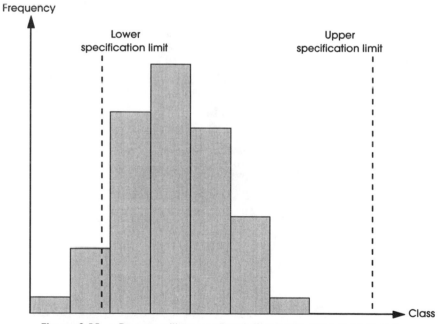

Figure 8.11.   Process with a small variation width, but not centered.

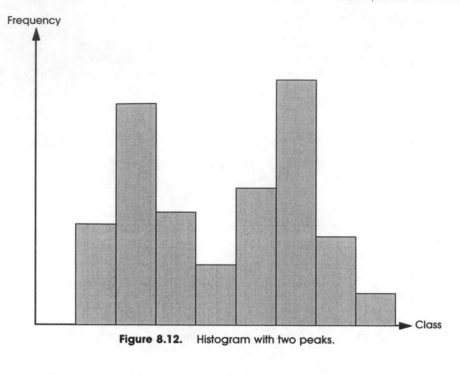

Figure 8.12.   Histogram with two peaks.

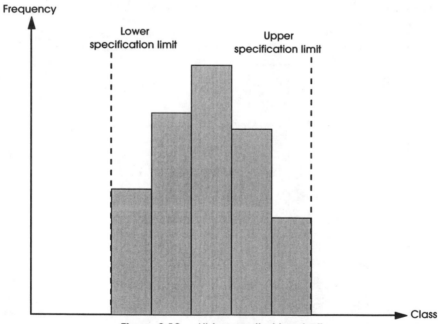

Figure 8.13.   Histogram that is cut off.

8.5   Relations Diagram

A relations diagram is a tool to identify logical cause-and-effect relationships in a complex and confusing problem or situation. For problems or situations where there is a network of such relationships, a relations diagram is particularly useful, as it has the ability to visualize them. There are two types of relations diagrams:

- Qualitative relations diagram
- Quantitative relations diagram

8.5.1 Qualitative Relations Diagram

In this type of diagram, both the problem and causes at several levels can be included, as shown in Figure 8.14. This way, the diagram is actually quite similar to the traditional cause-and-effect chart, but is more suited for complex problems (Rolstadås, 1995).

To generate a qualitative relations diagram, follow these steps:

1. Isolate all factors believed to be related to the problem.

2. Without forming an opinion about the relationships between the factors, each of these is freely expressed on an individual basis. Boxes can very well be drawn that contain the factors.

3. Identify the causal relationships between the factors and illustrate these with the help of arrows in the diagram.

4. Classify the factors depending on which role they play in the cause-and-effect situation.

5. Concentrate the improvement effort around the main causes for the problem.

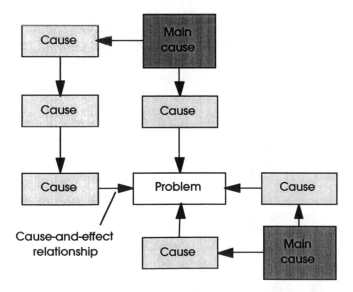

Figure 8.14. The principles of a qualitative relations diagram.

Relations diagrams can also be designed by using PC software. One such program is called PFT for Windows and can help the user in designing a number of different charts and diagrams.

After having spent much time and money on introducing a system for performance measurement, a company experienced that the system was not widely used and was viewed with little respect among the employees, at times even directly sabotaged. The company spent quite some time on constructing the relations diagram in Figure 8.15, and found two main causes for the problem.

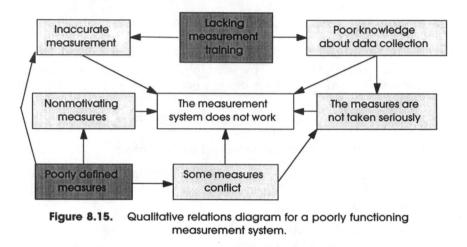

Figure 8.15.   Qualitative relations diagram for a poorly functioning measurement system.

8.5.2 Quantitative Relations Diagram

This variant of the relations diagram was originally developed in connection with the tool of benchmarking, which is described in chapter 10, and then particularly to determine which of a number of performance measures impacted others and which were impacted (Andersen and Pettersen, 1996). A quantitative relations diagram can, however, also be used for more general purposes than just classifying performance measures. Unlike the qualitative relations diagram, where an evaluation is made of relationships between factors, a somewhat simpler numerical approach is used to determine the role of different factors.

In Figure 8.16, a principal diagram is shown, constructed according to the following approach:

1. Place the factors to be included in the analysis throughout the diagram, preferably in a coarse circular shape.

2. For each factor, an assessment is made of which factors this impacts or is impacted by, and indicate these impacts with arrows. The direction of the arrow will then indicate the direction of the impact—that is, an arrow pointing away from factor A to factor B means that factor A impacts factor B.

3. After all relationships have been assessed, the number of arrows pointing into and away from each factor is counted and denoted in the diagram.

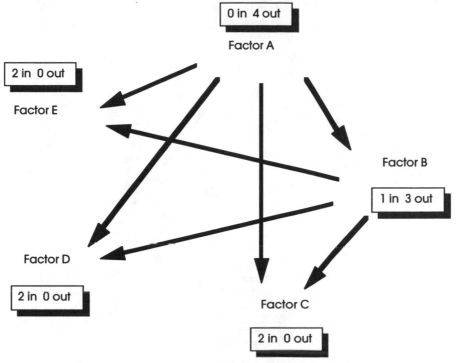

Figure 8.16.   A general quantitative relations diagram.

Depending on the number of arrows pointing in each direction for a factor, it can be defined to play one of two roles:

- Performance driver or cause—that is, a factor that impacts or enables the performance level of another factor. A different term is throttle variable. A performance indicator has more arrows pointing away from it than into it.

- Result indicator or effect—that is, a factor that indicates a consequence as a result of a performance driver. A result indicator has more arrows pointing into it than away from it.

When trying to find the main cause of a problem or an effect, alternatively wanting to identify the factor that will increase the performance if it is improved, the performance drivers must form the starting point. They drive the process and thus create the performance level of it.

If a quantitative relations diagram was used in the preceding example instead of a qualitative one, the result would be as depicted in Figure 8.17. This diagram gives the same information (that is, that the main problem is that the measurement system does not work [7 in, 0 out], while the main performance drivers are poorly defined measures [0 in, 5 out] and lacking measurement training [0 in, 3 out]).

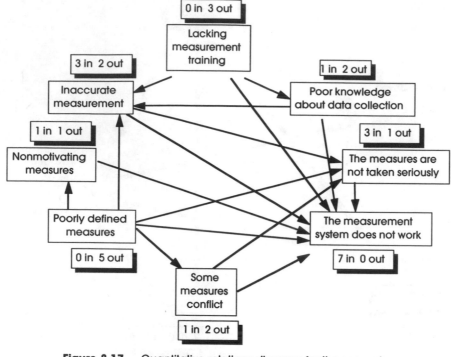

Figure 8.17.   Quantitative relations diagram for the example.

8.6   Matrix Diagram

So far, we have looked at tools that in different ways contribute to identifying relationships between different factors, often in the shape of cause-and-effect relationships.
The matrix diagram has about the same objective, but the force of this tool compared
to many of the others lies in its ability to graphically portray the strength of such relationships. As for many of the other tools, this one can also be used in several of the
stages in the improvement work, both to prioritize improvement areas, identifying
problems and causes, as well as planning.

Depending on the shape of the matrix, and thus the number of variables analyzed,
there are several types of matrix diagrams, as shown in Figure 8.18 (Swanson, 1995):

- The roof-shaped, which was briefly treated during the chapter about improvement planning using QFD (chapter 5). In this matrix, the relationships between
  the single elements of one variable are analyzed. For example, the degree of
  correlation between the individual performance measures was analyzed in the
  roof matrix in Figure 5.15. Unlike the other types of matrix diagrams, where
  the strength of the relationships are given in only one direction, the relationships in the roof matrix are classified as either neutral, positive, or negative.

- L-shaped

- T-shaped

- Y-shaped

- X-shaped

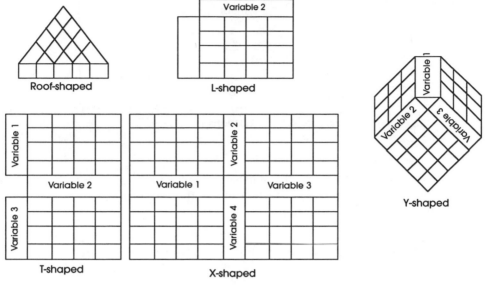

Figure 8.18. Types of matrix diagrams.

- In addition, there is a C-shaped matrix that treats three-dimensional relationships, but is very rarely used due to the complexity it entails.

The number of variables analyzed in the different formats, as well as the number of direct and indirect (that is, through a third variable) relations, are summarized in Table 8.4.

As explained in chapter 5, a standard set of symbols is used for indicating the strength of relations between variables. Figure 8.19 shows these symbols with the corresponding weight factors.

The steps when using a matrix diagram are:

1. Select the variables to be analyzed for potential relationships.

2. Select the matrix format based on the number of variables and the number of expected relations. To aid this task, use Table 8.4.

3. Insert the variables into the diagram.

Matrix shape	Number of variables	Direct relations	Indirect relations
L	2	1	0
T	3	2	1
Y	3	3	0
X	4	4	2
C	3	3 simultaneously	0
Roof	1	—	—

Table 8.4. Formats with the number of variables and relations for matrix diagrams.

Relation	Symbol	Weight
Weak	△	1
Medium	○	3
Strong	◉	9

Figure 8.19.   Relations symbols.

4. Indicate relations by using the symbols in Figure 8.19. Do not be tempted to use to corresponding weight factors inside the actual matrix, as this reduces the readability of the diagram.

5. For each row and column in the diagram, the corresponding weight factors for each relations symbol are summarized and the sums are presented in the diagram.

6. Variables with a high sum play an important role in the situation and should be analyzed further.

As with the relations diagram, matrix diagrams can be drawn be the help of computer software—for example, FPT for Windows.

The video rental chain described in a previous example wanted to assess the impact of the different business processes with regard to customer needs and expectations. The analysis was performed in an L-shaped matrix diagram, as shown in Figure 8.20.

Based on the diagram, the company could answer a number of questions. If, for example, it wanted to improve the check-out time, the relevant processes would be the check-out process itself as well as the information system used. Low prices, on the other hand, could be achieved through improvements in almost all processes.

Customer expectations	Processes							Total
	Market analysis	Check-out	Title selection	Adver-tising	Competitor analysis	Information system	Train-ing	
Low prices		△	○	○	◉	○	○	22
Good selection	◉		◉	○	△	○	◉	34
Several copies	◉		◉			○		21
Store layout		◉			○			12
Store location					○			3
Speedy check-out		◉				◉	○	21
Friendly staff		○					◉	12
Total	18	22	21	6	16	18	24	125

Figure 8.20.   Matrix diagram for the video rental chain.

REFERENCES

Andersen, Bjørn, and Per-Gaute Pettersen. *The Benchmarking Handbook: Step-by-Step Instructions*. Chapman & Hall, London, England, 1996.

Rolstadås, Asbjørn, ed. *Performance Management: A Business Process Benchmarking Approach*. Chapman & Hall, London, England, 1995.

Swanson, Roger C. *The Quality Improvement Handbook: Team Guide to Tools and Techniques*. Kogan Page, London, England, 1995.

CHAPTER 9

Tools for Idea Generation and Consensus Solutions

The two preceding chapters described tools for two somewhat related stages of the task of understanding the problems and the causes for them, related to a performance level below what is desired for the business process to be improved. The knowledge about the problems and their causes must at the next stage be used to generate solutions that can be implemented to achieve improvements. This chapter therefore describes some tools that can be used to generate ideas and aid the reaching of consensus solutions:

- Brainstorming
- Brainwriting/Crawford slip method
- Nominal group technique
- Affinity chart

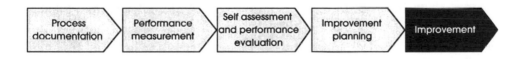

9.1 Brainstorming

Finding a solution to the problems we are usually faced with in improvement projects requires creativity. Most of us are usually far better at thinking analytically to find *the* right solution. In improvement work, the purpose is to find as many solutions as possible that can contribute in the right direction and then possibly only proceeding with the most promising ones. For this purpose, brainstorming and other related techniques described in this chapter are invaluable.

Brainstorming is a technique for idea generation (Rolstadås, 1995) that:

- Stimulates creativity
- Encourages joint problem-solving

- Makes it possible for the participants to build on one another's ideas

- Minimizes the tendency to prematurely evaluate ideas

- And not in the least, appreciates thinking that expands the traditional boundaries of the solution space

There are two different ways to brainstorm:

- Structured brainstorming, where the individual participant in turn launches one idea. This approach is the one that is most structured and ensures equal participation, but is less spontaneous and to some extent limits the possibility for building on one another's ideas.

- Unstructured brainstorming, where everyone can freely launch ideas all the time. This approach is very spontaneous, but is often more confusing and can lead to one or a few persons ending up dominating the activity.

The procedure is as follows:

1. Define clearly the topic of the brainstorming and write it on top of a white board or flip chart.

2. Let the participants launch ideas according to the approach used, structured or unstructured. Encourage everyone to launch ideas, no matter how silly they might seem.

3. Write down every single idea launched, preferably using the same wording as the original proposition.

4. It is not allowed to discuss, criticize, or evaluate ideas during the brainstorming itself. If an idea is not lucid enough to give any meaning, further explanation can be solicited.

5. Allow one recess or one period when the flow of ideas stagnate; it will usually pick up again. When the ideas seem to become only reformulations of previously launched ideas or when the frequency of new ideas is decreasing for the second time, close the process.

6. In the end, the ideas are evaluated. This can often be started by picking the obviously good ideas, the so-called "stars." The rest of the ideas can be sorted into groups, either by theme or by decreasing potential.

The consolidated list of ideas will now form a very suitable starting point for the task of defining the improvement projects to be started. While brainstorming is all about being creative and relaxed and flexible, one can use software for guiding and recording the brainstorming. One such highly acclaimed program is ParaMind.

Also remember the established rules for brainstorming:

- No criticism or discussion of ideas is permitted during the brainstorming.

- Laugh *with* crazy ideas, not *at* them.

- Be loose and spontaneous; there are no stupid ideas.

- Keep all ideas.

- Combine ideas. The ideas are not mine or yours; they are the group's.

9.2 Brainwriting/Crawford Slip Method

These are the names of two similar methods for conducting a brainstorming in writing. The advantage of a written idea generation approach is that it is easier to describe more detailed and coherent ideas, which often leads to the development of equally coherent solutions. While brainwriting is almost solely a written adaptation of brainstorming, the Crawford slip method is a technique that also protects the anonymity of the participants. This last approach is therefore often used when the group that will generate ideas experiences conflict that stifles creativity or when large amounts of information are expected to surface through the generating session (Swanson, 1995).

Looking at brainwriting first, it can be performed in two different ways:

- The card method, where the ideas are written on small cards and circulated among the participants for addition of related ideas or extension with other elements.

- The gallery method, where ideas are written on a number of white boards or flip charts and the participants circulate among these to add related ideas or expand on existing ones.

The procedure for brainwriting is as follows:

1. As with brainstorming, start by clearly defining the target topic for the idea generation. The topic is either written on a white board or on the participants' individual cards if the card method is used.

2. The participants then write down their ideas, either on the cards or on their white board. Precise formulations are encouraged, while still being sufficiently detailed to enable understanding without explanations from the owner.

3. The participants are allowed to add to others' ideas to reap effects from combining ideas or further developing them.

4. In the end, the ideas are verbally discussed by the groups and preferably also sorted into classes of ideas.

The Crawford slip method must be seen as a variant of the card method, where the cards are not circulated for extending others' ideas. Neither is an open evaluation of the ideas conducted, which further increases the requirements for accurate idea formulation. Sorting the ideas is done by one person, often aided by computer software designed for this purpose, several of which are offered on the market. The final document that summarizes all ideas can in the end be used openly in the group to reach agreement on which ideas will be used further in the improvement work.

9.3   Nominal Group Technique

As mentioned during the description of brainstorming, it might be a problem that the loudest persons in the group dominate such an activity. An unfortunate effect of this, besides the fact that the full potential for ideas of the group is not realized, is that those who feel they have been overlooked will later on not commit to the produced conclusions. The intention of nominal group technique, often abbreviated NGT, is to render possible a brainstorming where all participants have the same vote when selecting solutions.

To use NGT, the following steps are recommended:

1. As in brainwriting, the first step is written idea production where each person generates ideas and writes these on so-called idea cards, one idea on each card.

2. All the produced ideas are registered on a flip chart and the ideas briefly discussed. The purpose is to clarify the content of each idea as well as eliminate similar ideas. In the end at this stage, each idea is assigned a letter from A and onward.

3. The next step is again an individual activity, where the participants rank the ideas. From the complete list of ideas, each participant can select up to five ideas that are written on their ranking card. Each idea is identified using the assigned letter from the list on the flip chart. When ranking ideas, the participants assign points to the ideas, from 5 for the most important/best idea and down to 1 for the least important/good idea.

4. The session leader collects the ranking cards and writes down the assigned points on the flip chart. For each idea, the points are summarized to total scores. The idea achieving the highest total score is the group's prioritized idea or solution.

In the ensuing improvement work, it will be logical to start with the solution achieving the highest score or the two or three most important ones.

A company of about 400 employees experienced grave delays in the internal communication between individuals and departments. Normal brainstorming sessions produced some good ideas, but far from everyone participating launched any ideas. NGT was therefore used next, and after having collected the individually generated ideas, the list looked like this:

    A. Introduce/extend the use of electronic mail.

    B. When receiving a query, feedback should be given that the query has been received.

    C. Develop routines for informing about employees changing offices.

    D. System for telephone messages when traveling.

    E. Weekly department meetings and meetings across departments.

    F. Automatic mail sorting.

    G. Rebuilding the office area into an office landscape.

H. Compulsory table rotation during lunch breaks.

The ranking card of one of the participants is portrayed in Figure 9.1, while the resulting flip chart list is shown in Figure 9.2. The result was that the company introduced an electronic mail system giving absolutely everyone access to e-mail and training to use it.

Ranking card NGT	
Problem: Poor internal communication	
Idea	Points
A	5
B	4
C	1
D	2
H	3

Figure 9.1.   Individual ranking card.

Nominal group technique		
Problem: Poor internal communication		
Idea	Points	Total
A	5 5 4 5 3 2 5 4	33
B	4 3 4 3 2 2	18
C	1 4 5 3 5	18
D	2 3 4 5 2 2 3	21
E	1 2 1	4
F	2 3 2 4 1	12
G	1 5 3 2 1	12
H	3 5 5 5 1	19

Figure 9.2.   Resulting flip chart list.

9.4   Affinity Chart

This tool is known by several names, including the KJ chart. KJ are the initials of the inventor of the predecessor of the tool, the KJ method, by Jiro Kawakita, a Japanese anthropologist. The purpose of the tool is to create relationships between seemingly unrelated ideas, conditions, or meanings. This is done by grouping visual data points and finding underlying relationships connecting the groups. It is typically a creative technique that requires an open mind on the part of the participants (Aune, 1993).

The steps to construct an affinity chart are:

1. The participants are gathered in a room with a large white board. The topic to be analyzed is written in a large font at the top of the board, preferably in neutral terms, and underlined.

2. Ideas or solutions are brainstormed and written on adhesive notes. These should be briefly and succinctly formulated, but never only as one single word. The notes are attached to the board in a totally random pattern.

3. In silence, without any discussion, the group should try to move the notes around to form groups of ideas that are related. It is usual that the notes are moved back and forth many times before they find their places. Depending on the number of ideas, this might easily take an hour or more. The alternatives are to either set a time limit or letting the board stay for a longer period of time (for example, an entire working day, several days, or a week), and letting the participants stop by and move the notes as new impulses surface.

4. After having completed the grouping, the participants discuss the final shape of the chart. As the motives for placing notes in specific spots are explained, minor movements might be in order and should be allowed. The total number of groups should not exceed five to ten. The most important task at this step is, however, to make titles for the groups. Large groups can be divided into subgroups at lower levels.

5. Next, the chart itself is drawn by drawing boxes around the groups and possibly by adding arrows between them to indicate further relationships than demonstrated by the grouping.

6. The last step is to evaluate the chart with regard to further effort. The groups contain elements and suggestions to problems and solutions that must be expected to affect each other, and thus must be seen in connection when defining improvement projects.

If one wants assistance in drawing such a chart, software can be used (for example, PFT for Windows).

A library decided to try the affinity chart among the librarians after having received many negative responses from customers about the quality of the service delivered. Six librarians of different age and belonging to different departments formulated the topic to be dealt with to be things that could be done to enhance the satisfaction among the library clients. After conducting a round of brainstorming on this topic, the board looked like Figure 9.3.

After having tried to group the notes for about an hour, the group realized they would not be able to complete it during that session, not in the least because the brainstorming had taken much energy and creativity. The board was therefore left for two days, and they often came by to move the notes around a little. The resulting affinity chart is shown in Figure 9.4. The arrows in the chart indicate relationships between elements that were not possible to place in the same group. This exercise both helped generate possible measures as well as group them into clusters of naturally related ideas. The further work was concentrated around one group of ideas at the time.

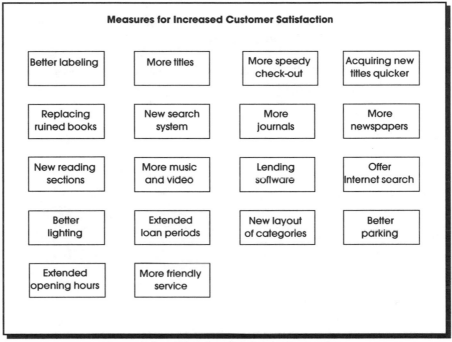

Figure 9.3. Ideas in a totally random pattern.

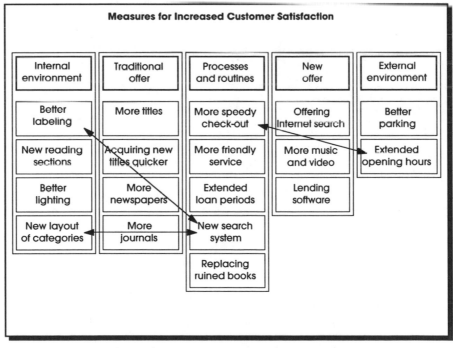

Figure 9.4. Grouping according to affinity.

REFERENCES

Aune, Asbjørn. *Kvalitetsstyrte bedrifter* (the title translates to *Quality-Managed Companies*). Ad Notam, Oslo, Norway, 1993.

Rolstadås, Asbjørn, ed. *Performance Management: A Business Process Benchmarking Approach*. Chapman & Hall, London, England. 1995.

Swanson, Roger C. *The Quality Improvement Handbook: Team Guide to Tools and Techniques*. Kogan Page, London, England, 1995.

CHAPTER 10

Tools for Improvement

The categories of tools that have been presented so far have been classified as suited for problem understanding, problem analysis, idea generation, and so on. The main purpose of these has always been to contribute to improvement, even if they only cover a smaller portion of the total activity leading up to this target. The tools presented under the heading of improvement are at the outset more directly geared toward this purpose. As has been mentioned already, the dividing lines between the categories are not crystal clear. The tools presented here are:

- Streamlining

- Idealizing

- Quality function deployment

- Work unit analysis

- Statistical process control/control chart

- Business process reengineering

- Benchmarking

10.1 Streamlining

The main principle behind streamlining is to trim away excess waste and superfluous elements in business processes. An aspect of a streamlined process is that it flows easily, without resistance lowering the performance level, neither internally within the process, nor in its interaction with the environment within which it exists. To achieve this streamlining effect, there are several tools that can be used in isolation, but, when put together, produce a much higher effect. Some of these are briefly presented in the following; they are presented in the order in which they are recommended when streamlining a business process (Harrington, 1991).

10.1.1 Bureaucracy Elimination

The words *streamlined* and *bureaucratic* are quite opposite. *Streamlined* is usually associated with a process that is efficient and flows easily; *bureaucracy* is synonymous with a process that is slow and cumbersome. Bureaucracy is often an obstacle on the way toward process thinking and the transition from departmental to process management. A first natural step when streamlining business processes is therefore to eliminate bureaucracy.

The typical effect of bureaucracy is unnecessary paper work. Managers often spend 40 to 50 percent of their time writing or reading job-related material. Studies have shown that approximately 60 percent of all office work in a company consists of reviewing others' work and storing and retrieving information, sometimes useful and very often not useful information. The negative effects of this are many and often impossible to measure. A critical review of all such bureaucratic tasks is therefore important, for the clear purpose of minimizing all delays, red tape, and other operations that do not stand out as useful, value-adding, or as supporting other processes.

One possible approach to eliminating bureaucracy is:

1. To start, the bureaucracy must be tracked down. Bureaucracy is often identified by asking questions like:

   - Is the activity performed to inspect or approve someone else's work?

   - Does it require more than one signature?

   - Are several copies made of the result?

   - Are several copies stored for no apparent reason?

   - Are copies sent to persons who do not need or use them?

   - Are persons or departments involved that stifle efficiency and quality of the work?

   - Another good clue to bureaucracy is unlimited use of the copier or access to large filing cabinets. Studies have shown that about 90 percent of all documents stored in an organization are never used again.

2. By combining the flow chart for the process and the answers to the questions above, activities that constitute bureaucracy are colored blue—that is, the activities that are connected to review, approval, signing, or inspection.

3. The person responsible for each of the "blue" activities is asked to present an overview of time and costs related to the activity as well as its usefulness. This usually meets some resistance, as all such activities are viewed as essential for the daily operation and long-term survival of the organization. Referring to a study undertaken in an American company, it might still be possible to persuade people to do so. A request for the purchase of equipment exceeding a certain amount of dollars had to go through five administrative levels for approval. Of ten requests sent for review, two only contained the right cover page allotting space for these signatures and the rest were purely blank pages.

Together with the other eight, these two passed right through the system and were duly approved.

4. Activities that cannot be justified are eliminated.

10.1.2 Redundancy Elimination

Especially for administrative processes, it is true that many identical or similar activities often are performed at two or more places in the process. This particularly occurs when different departments or different organizations in the supply chain perform their tasks independently and without knowing what the others do. This increases the process costs, but also brings along an increased likelihood that conflicting data exist. An example is a case where the purchasing department solicits prices for a component, while the design department does the same, but is quoted a different price. At different places in the organization, these data are used, which causes inaccuracy and errors. Due to lacking trust in many organizations, each person and each department often keeps their own records over matters like absenteeism and overtime. At the same time, this is done centrally, and the information in the two systems often differs.

The costs this double record-keeping entails and the problems caused by conflicting data must be avoided. For this purpose, there are really no easy tricks, beyond going through each of the activities and results associated with the process, with the intention of identifying and eliminating activities, documents, and other results that are generated more than once.

10.1.3 Value-added Analysis

Value-added analysis is a central concept in the streamlining of processes. Let us first study the concept of *value* and *value-added*. When a product passes through the company and is transformed from raw material into finished goods, two things really happen to its value:

- By supplying materials, labor, energy, and so on, the process incurs costs for the organization. The added value experienced by the product is, however, independent of these costs.

- By adding to the product qualities like functionality, aesthetics, brand name, and so on, the product experiences an added value that makes it possible to sell it for a (hopefully) higher price than the collective costs the process has incurred.

The challenge facing the organization is to ensure that the value of the product, expressed in terms of what the market is willing to pay for it, is higher than the costs for manufacturing it. This way, value is actually a theoretical concept that expresses both market value and true material value. An expression for the added value, AV, is:

$$AV = V_a - V_b$$

where V_a is the value after processing and V_b is the value before processing. As already mentioned, value in this sense is affected by a number of more subjective factors like functionality for the intended use, prestige, synergy with other products, and so on. Furthermore, this value for the customer is independent of how much it costs to manufacture the product. If it were possible to manufacture a Mercedes for half the current costs, the value for the customer would still be the same.

During the processing of the product within the organization, it is made subject to a number of activities. These can be divided into three categories:

- Real value-adding activities (RVA)—activities that from the end customer's point of view add value to the product. These are the typical transforming operations that create the product's functionality and appearance.

- Organizational value-adding activities (OVA)—activities that from the customer's point of view do not add any value, but that are necessary from the organization's point of view. These can be production planning, maintenance, personnel administration, and so on.

- Non value-adding activities (NV)—activities that neither from the customer's, nor from the organization's point of view add any value at all. Typical examples are waiting, storing, reworking, and so on.

Value-added analysis includes an analysis of each single activity in the processes to determine their contribution to the added value for the end customer. The intention is to classify all activities as one of these three types and then work to optimize OVA and eliminate NVA. The analysis is carried out as shown by the sequence of questions in Figure 10.1 (Harrington, 1991).

After having classified each activity in the process as one of these three categories, markers are used to color them in the flow chart. RVA are marked green, OVA yellow, and NVA red. This gives a good overview of the portion of activities that are truly value-adding. Such a picture can often shock the organization. Very often, less than 30 percent of the incurred costs are spent on RVA, while less than 5 percent of the time

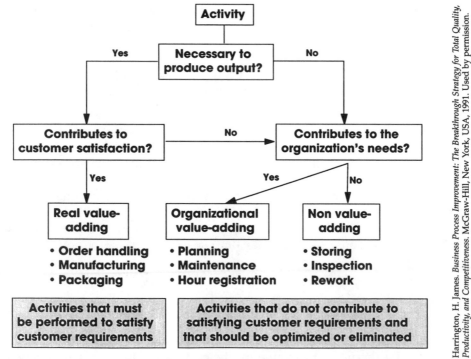

Harrington, H. James. *Business Process Improvement: The Breakthrough Strategy for Total Quality, Productivity, and Competitiveness.* McGraw-Hill, New York, USA, 1991. Used by permission.

Figure 10.1.   Value-added analysis.

consumed belongs to RVA. Another way of portraying this information is by using a so-called cost-cycle time chart, as shown in Figure 10.2 (Harrington, 1991). The chart shows the effects that can be achieved by eliminating NVA and minimizing OVA, in order to let RVA constitute the main part of the process's time and costs.

The core task of removing NVA and minimizing OVA is a project of its own for which there are no general answers as to how should be performed. Some general advice, on the other hand, is:

- Rework can only be eliminated by eliminating the source causing the error to occur in the first place.

- Pure movement of documents or other information can be minimized by combining operations, moving people closer to each other, or by automation.

- Waiting time can be minimized by combining operations, balancing the work load, or automation.

- Most output from NVA can be eliminated if management accepts it.

- Inspection and control can be eliminated by changing policies and procedures.

The result should be, as already mentioned many times, an increase in the portion of RVA, a reduction in the portion of OVA, and a minimization of the portion of

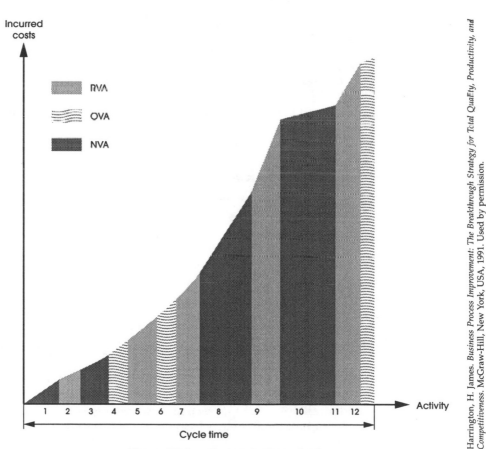

Figure 10.2. Cost-cycle time chart.

Harrington, H. James. *Business Process Improvement: The Breakthrough Strategy for Total Quality, Productivity, and Competitiveness.* McGraw-Hill, New York, USA, 1991. Used by permission.

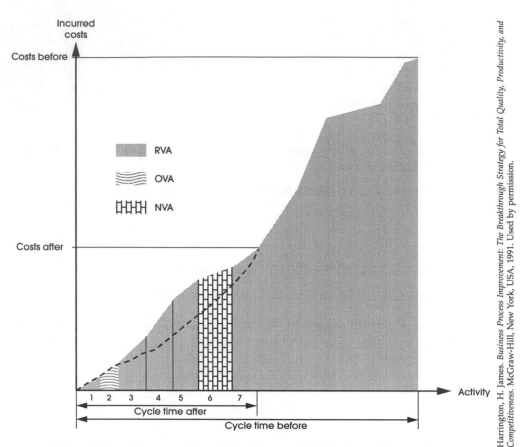

Harrington, H. James. *Business Process Improvement: The Breakthrough Strategy for Total Quality, Productivity, and Competitiveness.* McGraw-Hill, New York, USA, 1991. Used by permission.

Figure 10.3.   Corresponding chart after completed value-added analysis.

NVA. After a typical value-added analysis, the resulting chart might look like the one in Figure 10.3 (Harrington, 1991).

10.1.4 Process Cycle Time Reduction

Critical business processes are subject to the rule of thumb that time is money. Such processes are usually carried out in critical resources that often are bottlenecks. At the same time, the products from these processes are the ones that really matter to the customers. Therefore, the products should be delivered to them as fast as possible. Long cycle require capacity of the critical resources for unnecessarily lengthy periods of time, they stifle efficient delivery to the customer, and they incur storage costs for the company.

To determine where the crusade against long cycle times should be started, consider activities that cause delays, activities that originally display a long cycle time, or particularly critical processes. Typical efforts to remedy long cycle times are:

- *Perform activities in parallel instead of in sequence.* Very often, most of the steps in a business process are performed in sequence, although they could just as well be carried out in parallel. A serial approach results in the cycle time for the entire process being the sum of the individual steps plus transport and waiting time between steps. When using parallel approach, the cycle time can be reduced by as much as 80 percent while producing a better result. A classic example is

product development, where the current trend is toward concurrent engineering. Instead of first making a concept, then drawings, then bill-of-materials, then processes, all activities take place in parallel in integrated teams. The development time is reduced dramatically, and the needs of all those involved are considered during the development process.

- *Change the sequence of activities.* This point is closely connected to unnecessary transport of documents and products. Very often, both documents and products are transported back and forth between machines, departments, buildings, and so on. For instance, a document might be brought back and forth between two offices a number of times for inspection and signing. If the sequence of some of these activities can be changed, it is perhaps possible to perform all processing of the object when it comes by the place for the first time.

- *Reduce interruptions.* Issues that cause long delays and increase the cycle time for critical business processes are *interruptions.* The production of an important order can, for example, be stopped by an order from a far less important customer, but one that has turned into a rush order because it has been delayed. Persons working inside critical business processes can be interrupted by phones that could very well have been handled by someone else. The main principle is that everything should be done to allow uninterrupted operation of the critical business processes and let others handle interruptions.

- *Improved timing.* Many activities are of such a nature that they are performed with relatively large time intervals between each activity. For example, there might be a report that is generated only once a week, or purchasing orders that are issued every other day. People using these reports should be aware of such deadlines to avoid missing them. Often, the manufacturing department does not know that purchasing requirements that are not reported by noon Thursday will not be purchased until the following week. Improved timing in these processes can save many days in cycle time.

There are certainly numerous other approaches suitable for reducing cycle times, but these are some of the most important ones. A concerted streamlining effort employing some or all of these techniques for streamlining will give the best result.

A manufacturer of electric appliances, after 25 years of continuous growth, had come to a point where many of the administrative business processes were cumbersome. Some important processes, especially order processing, had become so time-consuming that they inhibited further improvements in other operative processes. The company thus decided to try some of the techniques for streamlining this process.

As the company grew, a number of different computer systems had been installed, including an order system. However, when this system was installed, the old routines had simply been automated or transferred to an electronic format. These routines were designed for a much lower sales volume and complexity. The dominant opinion was that a large bureaucracy was being kept alive artificially, and that the first step was to identify and eliminate the elements of this bureaucracy.

The company was particularly interested in procedures and mechanisms where documents and decisions needed approval from one or more people or departments. An assessment of the system for order processing

revealed no less than 12 instances on an order's path from receipt to start of production where somebody had to approve someone else's work. An analysis of these 12 instances made it clear that they consumed nine days altogether. At the same time, only two of these was a true review undertaken before approval was given. Combined with frequent customer complaints about long order processing times, it was obvious that something needed to be done. At the 10 instances where no real review was performed, the operative people performing the original work were given authority to approve their own work. This saved seven to eight days on average and an unknown amount of money.

Furthermore, they knew that many subsystems had been connected throughout the years. Each of them performed the same or similar tasks. The logical step was therefore to perform a redundancy elimination. For this task, a detailed flow chart portraying the process and output from it was used. At closer inspection, 16 highly similar steps were found, mainly activities where different versions of order documents were generated. If one globally available order document were produced, 13 steps in the process could be removed immediately. Over a period of four months, the order system was totally redesigned to allow information to be entered once to be available to the entire organization. This both eliminated nine days of work and dramatically improved the quality and accuracy of the process and its output.

Finally, a value-added analysis was undertaken. The current process after having performed the two preceding analyses contained a very small portion of NVA. The portion of OVA was a little higher, but definitely not unreasonably high. By further cutting the time consumed by individual activities related to registering internal documents, this portion could be reduced further. Figure 10.4 and Figure 10.5 show the cost-cycle time charts

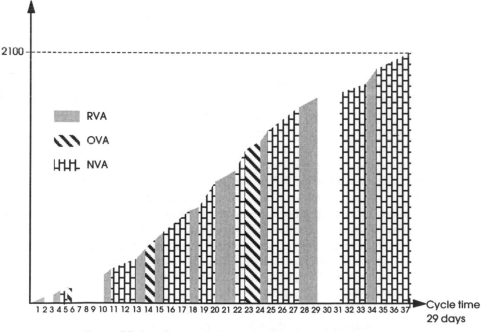

Figure 10.4.   Cost-cycle time chart for the original process.

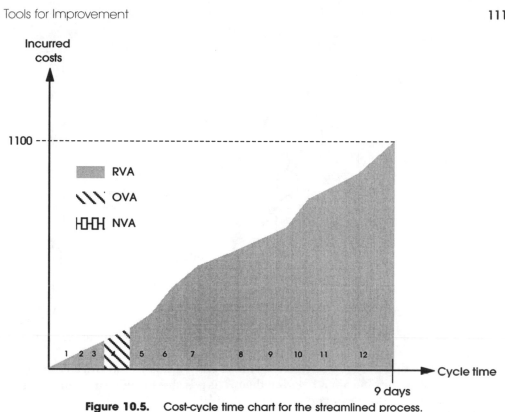

Figure 10.5. Cost-cycle time chart for the streamlined process.

for the original process and the streamlined process. The cycle time was reduced by about 19 days or 64 percent and the costs by about $1000 for a standard order.

10.2 Idealizing

Instead of starting from the existing process and analyzing its individual steps for potential efficiency gains, as in the value-added analysis, it is possible to free yourself from the limitations the current process imposes. This is the principle underlying *idealizing*. The purpose of this technique is to imagine how good the ideal process, without any form of waste or other inhibiting elements, could be. As a tool for generating possible solutions, this can at times be quite effective. Even if it is obvious that the ideal process cannot be implemented in practice, it can provide insight into how it should be implemented. The differences between the ideal process and the current situation can thus be used as a starting point for formulating solutions and improvement projects.

Idealizing is a typical group exercise, as numerous participants ensures that as many ideas as possible are captured. It is important that those performing the process are part of this group, as they are the ones daily dreaming of the ideal process. At the same time, people unfamiliar with practical limitations can also present refreshing ideas. Thus, a mixture should be included in the group.

Otherwise, there are really no specific guidelines on how to use or perform idealizing. Flowcharts can be to used in this work. After having constructed a flowchart for the ideal process, it is interesting to compare it to the chart for the current process. The powerful, graphic representation achieved by this approach is also a good starting

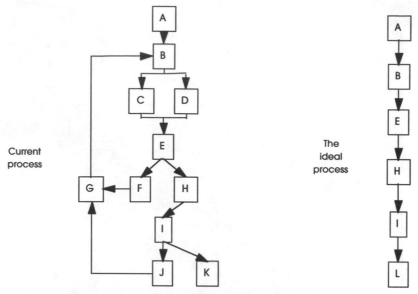

Figure 10.6.   Analysis of the current and ideal process in idealizing.

point for analyzing the gaps between the processes. Figure 10.6 shows an example of this. By studying the deviations between them, it is possible to define measures to move the process toward the ideal state.

Idealizing is, by the way, quite closely related to the so-called AΔT analysis, whose objective is slightly different. This tool is described in chapter 12.1.

A medium-sized printing company did a number of smaller jobs for different customers, typically printing advertising brochures, catalogues, and similar material. After having been troubled for a long time by errors in the finished printed material, it was decided to use idealizing to outline the ideal process that would ensure discovery of errors before actual printing. Seven persons from different functional areas in the company took on this job and had many shorter meetings during a period of two weeks. The resulting ideal process, as well as the old way of doing things, are shown in Figure 10.7.

The company spent the next three months moving toward this ideal process. Although, quite a lot remained before the ideal process was reached, not in the least due to the need for investments, the amount of errors not discovered before printing was reduced from on average 18 per month before the improvement work started to one potential error afterwards.

10.3 Quality Function Deployment

As was mentioned in chapter 5, quality function, or QFD, was originally used as a tool to facilitate customer-oriented product development. The core idea of QFD and how it is used for this purpose is partly described in chapter 5—at least to the extent

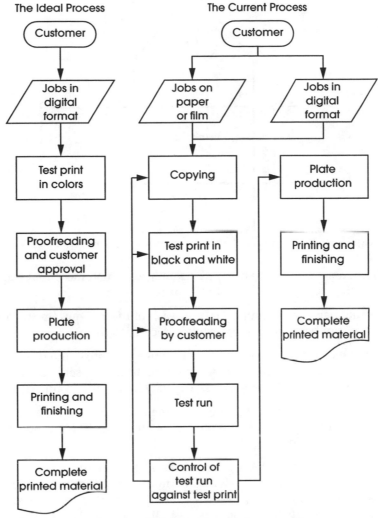

Figure 10.7. Idealizing in a printing company.

intended in this book, which does not aim to describe product development on its own. The focus of that description is how the tool of QFD can be used for improvement. The core of QFD is, however, so versatile that it can be applied for process improvement, as described in this chapter.

10.3.1 QFD as a Tool for Process Improvement

The most prominent feature of QFD is that it envisions relationships and connections between ends and means, as well as an analysis of these. This principle, along with the house of quality (see Figure 10.8), is utilized to identify improvement actions for a business process. Employed for this purpose, the meaning of the different fields in the house of quality are as follows:

- *What* expresses the requirement set for the process. The most important requirements are those that represent external customers, but also included are

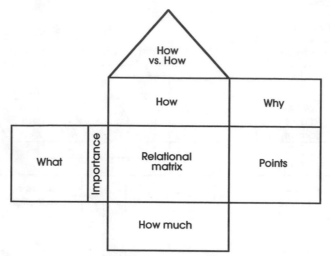

Figure 10.8.   The general house of quality, the chart used by QFD.

requirements from external suppliers, internal customers and suppliers, as well as other concerns internal to the organization.

- To separate between the importance of each of these requirements, the field of *Importance* can be used to assign weight factors to them.

- *How*, on the other hand, shows the means used to satisfy the different requirements. If one requirement is a short operation time for a service process, a mean could, for instance, be expanding the capacity in periods around demand peaks.

- In the *Relational matrix* in the middle of the chart, the relations between ends, or requirements in this case, and means are analyzed. The symbols used in this field are repeated in Figure 10.9.

- In the roof of the chart, that is, the *How vs. How* field, the connections between the different means can be analyzed. If another mean for the service process is staff reduction, motivated by the company's demands for reduced costs, the conflict between these two can easily be visualized in the roof. The corresponding symbols for the roof matrix are also repeated, as shown in Figure 10.10.

- In the same way as for products in the original use of QFD, the *Why* field can be used during process improvement to perform a simple benchmarking against other organizations' processes.

- Finally, the *How much* field is used to illustrate the results of the analysis. For each connection in the relations diagram, the importance factor for the requirements is multiplied by the weight factor for the relation, and the sum of these products for each requirement is placed in the *How much* field. The higher the score in this field, the more requirements can be satisfied by this mean.

As in the presentation of QFD for improvement planning, an example provides insight into the process improvement method. Figure 10.11 shows a resulting house of quality after QFD has been used to identify suitable improvement means for the business process of distribution from finished goods inventory.

Such an analysis will normally be undertaken by a group established to improve a specific process. The group has in this case identified requirements for the process that are posed both by the company's customers as well as internal demands. Each of

Relation	Symbol	Weight
Weak	△	1
Medium	○	3
Strong	◉	9

Figure 10.9.   Symbols for the relational matrix.

Relationship	Symbol
Strong positive	◉
Weak positivo	○
Weak negative	✕
Strong negative	✖

Figure 10.10.   Symbols for the roof matrix.

the requirements has been assigned an importance factor. For example, speedy and safe delivery are considered essential, while a low need for overtime and good overview are ranked quite low. The typical situation, which is completely in line with the norm, is that the external requirements count more than the internal ones.

Based on these requirements, the next step involved brainstorming a number of means or process features of the distribution process that were assumed to have a positive impact on the requirements. At each connection point between a demand and a process feature, an assessment was made as to what extent the mean impacts the requirement, which is denoted by the symbols used in the relations matrix. In addition, data for these requirements was collected or estimated for two competitors of the company. This information is presented in the *Benchmarking* field at the right-hand side. As can be seen, the company trails with regard to safe delivery, as both, but particularly competitor A, score very well. Targets have also been defined, mainly based on input from the competitors' performance levels and strategic decisions.

For each mean, it has been evaluated whether any relevant quantifiable targets could be defined. As the matrix reveals, a target was for example defined for the number of extraordinary repairs beyond ordinary maintenance for the distribution trucks, that is, less than one per 100,000 kilometers. However, far from every mean has had targets defined this way. Therefore, in the field below, an assessment on an objective scale has been made of the company's own performance level, that of the competitors, and the company's targets. For dependability of the trucks, for instance, the company is far behind the competitors, while the target of one repair per 100,000 kilometers is quite ambitious.

The correlation symbols in the relations matrix, or more correctly the weight factors for the symbols, are multiplied by the factors that represent the importance of each of the requirement elements. For each process feature, these products are summarized and placed in the field of absolute importance. The numbers in this field say something about to what extent an improvement in this individual process feature will impact the collective requirements. In the field immediately below, relative importance has been calculated, that is, how large a percentage of the total impact the single

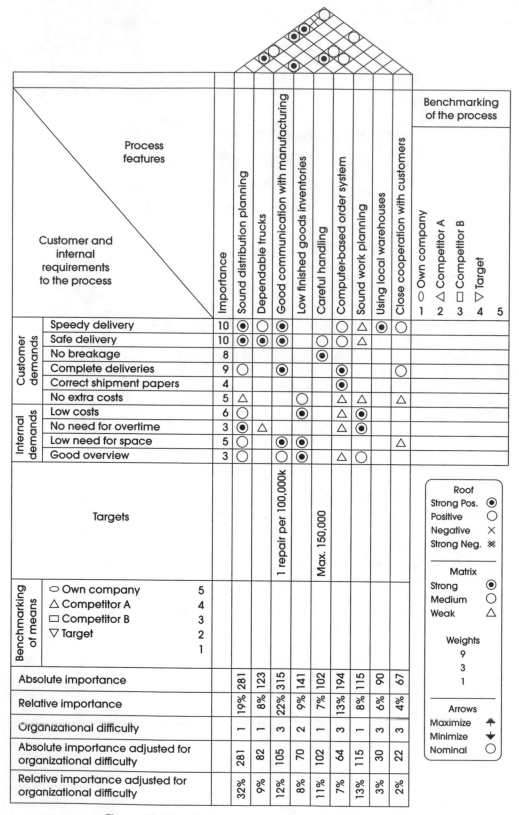

Figure 10.11. House of quality for process improvement.

process feature accounts for. Based on these calculations, we see that the three process features that stand out are sound distribution planning, good communication with manufacturing, and a computer-based order system.

Furthermore, a factor has been estimated that indicates how difficult it would be to implement the means in the organization. The higher the factor, the more difficulties are expected to be encountered. The importance values are divided by these factors, which give the corresponding importance figures, adjusted for organizational difficulty. If this aspect is included, it seems as if sound distribution planning is the process feature that has the highest ability to impact the requirements and the easiest implementation. This gives the company a clear sense of what element in the distribution process to improve. It probably also makes sense to include the mean that achieved the second-highest scores.

Finally, an evaluation has been performed in the roof of the house of quality with regard to synergy between the different means. If focusing on the distribution planning, we see that positive effects can also be expected from an improved communication with manufacturing and a computer-based order system. Local warehouses can, on the other hand, complicate the distribution planning task.

Even if this example does not capture all aspects of the use of QFD for improvement planning, it at least demonstrates how the volume of the voice of the customer can be turned up sufficiently to be heard when planning and evaluating improvement efforts. Expressing and appointing importance factors to the customer requirements maintains them throughout the entire process of assessments and calculations. Thus, the final prioritization, even if any direct links can be hard to see, will be highly influenced by them.

10.4 Work Unit Unalysis

It is arguable whether work unit analysis is a tool or an organizational mode. In this book, it will be viewed it as a tool, and therefore, it will be treated in this chapter. It is, however, also closely related to organizational principles, as dealt with in chapter 11.

The background for work unit analysis is the need for clear specifications to follow, no matter whether a physical product or a service is being generated, irrespective of whether this is for an internal or an external recipient. Too often, examples can be found of something being produced or a service being performed without having any clue to how the customer really wants it. Since this is how it has always been, things continue to be done the same way. The recipient spends much time changing what is received to the ideal format it should have been in, but does not ask the provider to change it, because it is believed to be impossible. This way, much unnecessary frustration and bother are created.

To clear up such silent misunderstandings and the lack of clear specifications that can be used as a yardstick for the quality, work units can be established and the interfaces between them analyzed. A work unit is defined as a group that performs a set of tasks and that constitutes a unit with well-defined inputs and outputs (Aune, 1993). For example, one person can be a work unit, but far more often, departments or parts of departments are defined as work units. According to the terminology used in this book, the obvious way of defining work units is to let those who perform separate segments of a business process form a work unit. Such a unit will always have suppliers and customers delivering and receiving input and output to and from the work unit (see Figure 10.12).

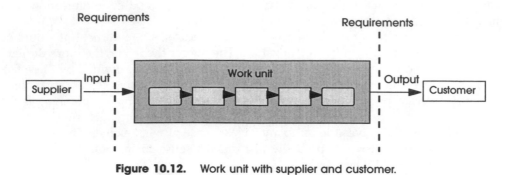

Figure 10.12. Work unit with supplier and customer.

Once such a work unit has been formed, it must, together with its suppliers and customers, define the requirements that:

- The work unit itself poses to the input from its suppliers, as well as performance measures to monitor whether they are satisfied.

- The customers pose to the output from the work unit and performance measures to monitor whether they are satisfied.

It is worth noticing that such an analysis is really intended to serve several purposes:

- First of all, a discussion around these requirements will bring to light the needs and demands of the different stakeholders, thus clearing up silent misunderstandings between supplier and customer.

- Furthermore, this analysis will lead to the establishment of clear performance measures that can be used for monitoring whether the quality of the input or output is good enough. This way, the supplier can be notified when the quality is starting to deteriorate and take action to counteract it.

- This analysis will ensure that as few items with defects or weaknesses as possible will be sent on for further processing, which is futile if the items must ultimately be discarded. If this applies to the last work unit before the item reaches the end customer, this will also prevent bad items from being shipped to the customer, where the defective item does even more harm than when eliminated internally.

The steps to conduct such a work unit analysis are:

1. The first logical step is to establish the work unit. If one attempted work unit cannot clearly define the input it receives and the output it delivers, the unit must be redefined, and most likely reduced.

2. To enable transmitting requirements from customers that also affect the suppliers of a work unit, the analysis should start at the customer end of the work unit. First, the unit's true customers must be identified. To do so, it is important to focus on the real products supplied by the unit, not feedback or some other communication delivered to others. Units performing physical production often have few customers while units supplying more administrative or

support services have many. The latter must, at least in the beginning, concentrate the analysis around the most important customers.

3. Once the customers have been mapped, the next step is to define, in close cooperation with them, the requirements that are set forth for the unit's output. It is important both to capture absolute demands and less articulated ones. This can be illustrated using the canoe model, as shown in Figure 10.13.

   The canoe model, named for the shape of the lines in the model (Akao, 1990), shows that there are several levels of customer requirements, and all should be kept in mind. The straight line of the figure portrays the clearly expressed requirements of the customer. Generally, these are the only demands the customer describes if being asked about his desires. If the customer is a potential car buyer, he could express requirements that the car should be spacious enough to seat five people comfortably, that the trunk should be so and so large, at least have a two liter engine, and include an RDS stereo for free.

   In addition, there exists a set of requirements that are so basic that they are not even expressed, as indicated by the lower curve. For the car buyer, these could be conditions that the car must be able to run easily 110–120 kilometers per hour, has a heater and wipers, steering wheel and four wheels, and that the paint is not scratched.

   Together, these two requirement sets constitute the complete set of demands posed by the customer to the supplier. This means that the work unit must be aware of both sets. The satisfaction level depends on how well both sets are satisfied. It is useless for a car to seat seven people very comfortably and have the best stereo available if the hood looks like a carving board. In other words, satisfying expressed requirements cannot rectify shortcomings in the basic demands. On the other hand, satisfying every single one of the basic requirements will not lead to complete satisfaction unless the expressed requirements

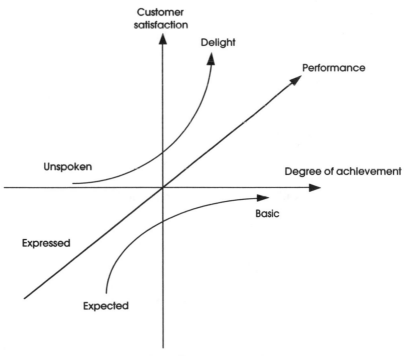

Figure 10.13. The canoe model.

are fulfilled. This will, at best, eliminate dissatisfaction. The danger is that the customer takes for granted that the supplier is aware of the basic requirements. Such silent assumptions are the main focus of the task of clarifying requirements in the work unit analysis.

The financial department of a large company produced weekly reports for the sales department containing the credit status of the customers. The responsible accountant put his heart into the accuracy of the report despite the time invloved and occasional delays. The sales department was not depending on precise accuracy, but on having the report on time, so as to be able to issue order confirmations at the agreed time. They assumed that the financial department understood this and did nothing to enlighten the accountants. Instead, they continued to be annoyed by the delayed reports, without appreciating the accuracy, and nothing got better.

When mapping the customer's requirements for a work unit's output, it is thus essential to capture both sets of demands, perhaps particularly the basic ones, as these do not always shine through. They will typically include issues like:

- Delivery frequency

- Deadlines

- Minimum quality requirements

- Basic product features

If these are captured and satisfied, the foundation for satisfaction should be sound. To further enhance satisfaction, and even delight the customer, we can examine a third set of requirements. *Requirements* is not really the correct word, because these are conditions not verbalized by the customer, and the customer is unaware of them himself. For the car buyer, this could include having the car delivered to his house, installing extra floor mats, pre-programming the radio and so forth. Once both the basic and expressed requirements have been fulfilled, the fulfillment of extra "requirements" can create true delight. This is often the little extra required to ensure buyer loyalty. The supplier should, however, keep in mind that once such extra requirements have been delivered, they are often added to the expressed or even basic requirements that must be fulfilled to avoid dissatisfaction.

4. After having completed the mapping of customers and output, the input and the suppliers must be mapped. Step 4 starts with the different input elements, while the suppliers are mapped in the next step.

5. Step 5 is then to map who supplies these input elements. Requirements must be defined for these, for which the canoe model is naturally also valid. This requirement description is produced in cooperation with the suppliers.

6. The next step is to map the processes performed by the work unit in order to transform input to output. For this task, flowcharts are a useful tool, as described in chapter 3.

7. Performance measures must be defined for these processes. Performance measures were treated in chapter 4, and their purpose is to enable the work unit to monitor and improve both customer satisfaction and internal efficiency/productivity. It is, by the way, important to limit the number of measures to an amount that can be actively followed up, preferably no more than five should be defined for a work unit.

8. Based on defined requirements and performance measures, the last step of the analysis is continuous measurement, generation of improvement suggestions, and implementation of these. Also the unit should repeat regularly the mapping of input and output requirements to capture changes in these.

A manufacturing company with about 400 employees was organized around traditional departments and displayed a normal distribution of responsibility among the departments. Based on incoming orders and prognoses generated by the sales department, the production planning department produced production plans and purchasing lists. These purchasing lists were sent to the purchasing department, which performed the actual procurement. To improve the interface between the production planning department and the other departments, a work unit was defined to consist of the five employees of the department. The scope of the unit was thus readily defined, and its purpose was equally clear, that is, to generate production plans and purchasing lists and monitor and follow up on these.

In the next phase, the work unit's customers were defined:

- The foreman in the component manufacturing department

- The foreman in the assembly department

- The purchasing department

- While the sales department was a supplier, it was also a customer receiving information

These were defined as the customers that received output directly from the work unit, even if there were more indirect customers, as for example the company's end customer, who in the end received the products for which the production was planned by the unit.

In cooperation with each of these internal customers, their requirements for the work unit's output were defined. Without going into detail, the different foremen had a number of demands pertaining to the accuracy of the plans, the workload, and sequential dependencies. The purchasing department had one requirement regarding the frequency of the purchasing list. Henceforth, it had been printed every Monday, which resulted in a high workload for the purchasing department early in the week, and a correspondingly low workload toward the week's end. Furthermore, deadlines for orders were sometimes missed that could have given earlier deliveries from the suppliers. Besides this, there were a number of requirements for the list, including how it should be sorted, its appearance, information included, and so on. The sales department's primary requirement was that when a request from a customer surfaced, an answer from the unit should be given very quickly about when delivery could take place, preferably with one day accuracy. Many of these conditions, especially toward the purchasing department, were previously unknown to the work unit, and this way, the analysis had already facilitated new discoveries.

Next, the input used by the production planning department in their planning work was mapped. This mainly consisted of two elements supplied by the sales and marketing department:

- Actual orders and sales prognoses

- Inventory status of component and finished goods inventories

The suppliers of the input were thus already well defined. When formulating the requirements for these two input elements, the work unit was surprised by some of the views of the suppliers. Regarding order and prognoses information, the work unit was depending on as current information as possible to plan the future workload in machines. It soon became clear that the sales department usually knew about a number of potential orders that would almost certainly become actual orders, which were never mentioned to the planning department. Similarly on the prognoses side, expected orders due to special campaigns in the stores were not included.

The two inventories kept a combination of manual and computer-based inventory records. Parts that were used in the manufacturing were registered on the computer, while sales of components as spare parts were first manually registered and then updated in the computer every second week. The work unit, which was also depending on accurate inventory information, did not realize this, which led to some unexplainable cases of missing parts.

This mapping on both the output and input side of the work unit immediately cued a number of changes and improvements that dramatically improved the conditions for all parties involved. Later on, performance measures were defined to measure the performance of the work unit. These were monitored every week, which led to even further improvements.

10.5 Statistical Process Control/Control Chart

A very practical characteristic trait of this world and the processes carried out in it, is that stabilized processes will display a logical statistical behavior. This means that the results from a process will normally fall within certain specifiable limits. This fact can be used for monitoring and improving an organization's processes.

10.5.1 Definitions of Variation

Before the actual tool of statistical process control, often abbreviated SPC, is presented, it is necessary to define some central terms in statistics. First of all, it is important to understand the difference between *chronic* and *sporadic variation*:

- *Chronic variation* is variation that is inherent in the process and is caused by a long line of factors, without one single cause for the deviation. It is, in other words, caused by something in the system. This variation is normal for the process and must be expected and lived with, unless the process itself is changed. If, for example, the time it takes to complete a mail route in a large office building is measured, it will invariably vary due to factors like the walking pace of the individual mail man, the number of letters to be delivered, the number and duration of breaks, the waiting time for elevators, and so on.

- *Sporadic variation* is caused by factors appearing infrequently and is often larger than the chronic variation. The deviation can usually be traced to one single cause, and can thus be eliminated by removing that cause. For the mail route, this could be variation caused by a freshly recruited mail man, incorrectly sorted mail, or an out of order elevator.

The purpose of statistical process control is to classify variation according to these two groups and thus facilitate further improvement of the process.

10.5.2 Basic Statistics

To understand the principles of SPC, it is absolutely essential to first understand the basic principles of statistics on which SPC is based. Most processes studied in an organization can be described reasonably accurately using two variables:

- The *arithmetic mean value* of the process measure being used, for example the diameter of a hole being drilled. The statistical term for this value is the *expected value*, and the expression for it is:

$$\overline{X} = \frac{1}{n} \sum_{i=1}^{n} X_i$$

- The *standard deviation* of the process, that is, a variable that says something about how much variation should be expected from the process. If we want to drill holes of diameter of 7.9 millimeter, that is, an expected value of 7.9, the standard deviation could be 0.15 millimeters. The symbol for the standard deviation is σ_x and the formula for calculating it is:

$$\sigma_x = \sqrt{\frac{\sum_{i=1}^{n} (X_n - \overline{X})^2}{(n-1)}}$$

Actually, it is not totally correct using the σ for the standard deviation. σ refers to the standard deviation for the distribution itself, while the standard deviation for the sample being taken is labeled s. This connotation has been used throughout the rest of the book.

If the observation or measurements of the process are distributed evenly around the expected value, we can use a so-called normal distribution to describe the process. This is often the case for stable processes. The normal distribution in statistical matters is a special distribution for several reasons:

- It is symmetric, that is, the likelihood of the process giving a result that is larger than the expected value is as high as for a result smaller than the expected value.

- If the distribution function graph is drawn, it looks like a bell, thus another term for this distribution is bell-shaped. Figure 10.14 shows a distribution

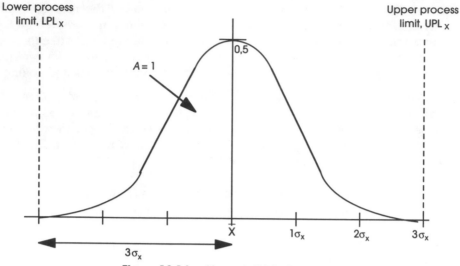

Figure 10.14.   Normal distribution curve.

curve, which expresses the likelihood that the process measure will assume a certain value.

- From the graph, it can be seen that the distribution curve crosses the *x* axis at two points, these points being respectively three times the standard deviation to the left of the expected value and equally far to the right of it. This means that the probability of getting a value that is less than the expected value minus three times the standard deviation or larger than the expected value plus three times the standard deviation, is practically zero. This is a basic quality of the normal distribution, namely that the maximum deviation that can be experienced lies within $3\sigma_x$. To be totally correct, 68,26 percent of all values will fall within one standard deviation, 95,45 percent within two, and 99,73 percent within three. The area below the distribution curve equals 1, which is another way of saying that all the probability is gathered within these limits of $\pm 3\sigma_x$.

Since all results from a process following this distribution are expected to fall within the total spread of six standard deviations, data that fall outside this area are sporadic deviations due to special causes. To monitor the process, so-called control charts are used that show the process limits of three standard deviations in each direction (see Figure 10.14) as well as the continuous measurements of the process. The construction of such charts is treated a little later.

When it comes to the quality of a process, it is generally better the narrower the chronic variation is. SPC is used to reduce this natural variation and to report occurrences of any sporadic variation for which the cause must be found. Before this is possible, the process must be statistically stable, that is, having a constant expected value and variation width.

Based on these simple statistical principles and related rules, it is thus possible to control a business process and discover whether the centering is changing, increasing variation width, variation beyond the expected limits, but also what normal variation must be expected. If a process measure lies far from the expected value, but within three times the standard deviation, it might be tempting to adjust it. But that introduces lopsidedness into the process, and in the future, deviations to the other side will occur. Attempts to rectify this by adjusting the process the other way usually moves the deviation to the other side. This evil circle that can result from adjusting processes that display only normal variation, is popularly termed *tampering*, and can be avoided by proper use of SPC.

Far from just physical, geometric measures related to manufacturing processes can be kept under statistic monitoring, even if many seem to think so. By using a number of different control charts, many different processes and process measures can be made subject to SPC:

- The time it takes to perform a task, physical or administrative.

- The costs incurred by a process, physical or administrative.

- The number of errors or defects produced by a process, physical or administrative.

- And obviously also specific geometric measures like length, diameter, and so on.

By defining control limits based on the expected and normal variation inherent in the process, continuous measures of the process' characteristic features are plotted in the chart. Depending on the results, different measures are taken. Which situations and which measures these are are discussed treated in detail in the section about interpreting control charts. Thus, SPC presents a powerful tool for monitoring and improving business processes.

10.5.3 Types of Control Charts

The normal distribution and how control limits can be based on three standard deviations is the simplest type of control charts. This type is not suited for all situations, however, thus other types have been defined. First of all, there is a difference between two basic types of variables:

- *Variable data,* that is, variables that are based on measurement, for example meters, hours, volts, and so on. These variables are measured on a continuous scale and with reasonably high accuracy.

- *Attribute data,* that is, variables measured by counting or classifying nonmeasurable characteristics (that is, acceptable/nonacceptable, brown/red, assembled/not assembled, and so on). Attribute data are quantified by integers or intervals of values. Variable data can also be converted to attribute data (that is, length by defining a limit for acceptable and nonacceptable).

For variable data, two charts must be used in pairs, one to control the centering of the process and one to control the variation width. For attribute data, on the other hand, only one chart is required.

Two weaknesses related to the use of a chart like the one shown in Figure 10.14 are as follows:

- The values that have been measured are not necessarily normally distributed, which renders the process limits uncertain.

- Such a chart is not very sensitive, as values within the process limits can be measured long after the process has changed its center or the variation width has increased.

This is usually remedied by using mean values for a group of measures instead of single values as the basis for the chart. The advantage in this is that mean values for a group of measures, almost regardless of the original distribution of the individual measures, approximately follow a normal distribution. Thus, the first weakness is avoided. At the same time, a chart based on such values is far more sensitive to changes in the centering of the process, which also counters the second weakness. In opposition to the process limits in charts based on single values, the limits in charts based on average values are termed *control limits*. The expected value for a mean variable consisting of the average *m* groups of single measures is then labeled:

$$\overline{X} = \frac{1}{m} \sum_{j=1}^{m} \overline{X}_m$$

The control limits are calculated by respectively subtracting and adding three times the standard deviation for the mean distribution. The standard deviation for a mean variable from a group of n individual values is calculated as follows:

$$s_{\overline{x}} = \frac{s_x}{\sqrt{n}}$$

There are seven chart types that are most frequently used, classified according to the variable that is being measured and the number of measurements that exist. These are shown Figure 10.15 and described in more detail after a brief overview (Swanson, 1995).

For variable data, there are three types of control charts:

- $\overline{X}$ and s, where the $\overline{X}$ chart plots the *mean value* for groups of measurements, while the s chart is used to monitor the variation width of the average measurements. The number of measurements in each group should normally be higher than ten.

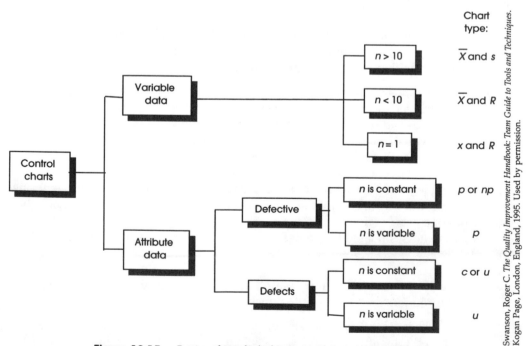

Figure 10.15.   Types of control charts and when to use them.

- $\overline{X}$ and R, where the $\overline{X}$ chart displays the same average measurements for the expected value. Both because the number of measurements in each groups often is lower than ten and because the term range, R, defined as the difference between the largest and smallest value in the group, is easier to understand than σ, an R chart is often used to monitor the variation width. For this reason, the chart pair $\overline{X}$ and s will not be described any further.

- x and R, where the x chart is based on the type of individual measurements first described, the type of chart that does not quickly detect changes in the process. The reason for occasionally using this chart is that the measurement costs are lower. At the same time, it may be the only alternative if the variable changes very quickly, which makes it impossible to make group measurements for example during a measurement of temperature. The variation width is controlled using an R chart, but in this case, R means the difference between the current and the previous measurement.

Before the charts of attribute data are presented, it is important to understand the differences between *defective* and *defects*. Defective items are scrapped because they do not satisfy the requirements, while defects are units that have some kind of weakness, but can be accepted because the specifications allow some degree of weakness. For attribute data, there are four chart types:

- np, which is used to monitor the number of defective items in a sample of constant size. The process measure used could be the number of defective cars manufactured in a day or the number of errors detected during order processing in a day.

- p, which is used for the number of defectives in samples of either constant or varying size.

- c, used to monitor the number of defects occurring in samples of constant size. Examples could be the number of errors in a five page document or the number of defects found on a circuit board.

- u, a more general variant of the c chart, which can also be used for samples of varying size.

Notice that the np chart plots values that cannot exceed the sample size, since only a portion of the items can be defective. Since the c and u charts are used for the number of defects, this number can very well exceed the sample size. The differences between defective and defects can be further illustrated by an example. When inspecting the surfaces of ten items, five items were found to have a total of eleven inconsistencies, while the other five were perfect. An np chart would have plotted five defectives if the specifications did not allow such inconsistencies. A c chart would plot eleven, as this was the total number of errors, but would not say anything about how many would have to be scrapped.

10.5.4 Constructing Control Charts

Under this heading, a general procedure for the use of statistical process control will be introduced. Afterwards, specific instructions will be given for calculating control limits for the different types of charts and how the charts are used.

Generally, when using SPC, the steps are:

1. Determine which type of data will be collected and controlled, that is, whether they are variable or attribute data, and also the expected number of samples.

2. Based on the guidelines of Figure 10.15, the suitable type of control chart is selected.

3. Collect the data required to calculate the control limits.

4. Construct the control chart by letting the y axis represent the variable being measured, and the x axis represents the process has been divided into measurement segments (time, subgroups, measurement number, and so on), and mark suitable intervals on the axes that make it easy to plot the measured values.

5. Calculate the lower and upper control limits and, where required, the mean and range of the data set. If one of the points falls outside the control limits, this point is removed and new limits calculated. If further points fall outside, the process is not statistically stable and the cause must be found and eliminated before the use of SPC can be continued.

6. Draw the control limits in the chart along with the existing measurements.

7. Continue plotting values as they are collected from the running process. The meaning of the points and necessary actions are interpreted based on the guidelines given in the next subchapter.

While this is a manual procedure for using statictical process control, many PC programs designed for quality improvement contain modules for constructing control charts. Two of these are SQCpack and NWA Quality Analyst. The rest of this subchapter is devoted to detailed guidelines for the construction of the individual chart types, except $\overline{X}$ and s, which will not be described any further.

$\overline{X}$ and R Charts

As mentioned, this is a pair of two charts, where the first focuses on the centering of the process, while the other controls the variation width. To construct such a chart pair, the following must be done:

1. Collect the data, typically more than 125 measurements of recent date are required.

2. Divide the data points into logical subgroups, where at least 25 subgroups are required to calculate the control limits. Subgroups should consist of data points that logically belong together, that is, are measured under the same conditions, close to each other in time. Usually, there will be two to five data points in each subgroup, which defines the sample size, n.

3. For each subgroup, the mean value, $\overline{X}$, and the range, R (that is, the difference between the largest and smallest value in the subgroup) are calculated. For the mean value, one more decimal place is used than in the measurements themselves.

4. Calculate the mean value for the entire data set, $\overline{\overline{X}}$, either by averaging all the individual measurements or averaging the calculated means for the subgroups.

Here, two more decimal places should be used than in the original measurements. This value will represent the center line of the $\overline{X}$ chart.

5. Calculate the average range, $\overline{R}$, by finding the mean of all the range values calculated in step 3. This value represents the center line of the R chart.

6. Calculate the control limits for both charts. To simplify the calculations, calculation factors have been developed that correspond to a deviation of $\pm$ three standard deviations for sample sizes from one to ten (see Table 10.1). For larger sample sizes, an $\overline{X}$ and s chart should be used. Notice that for all subgroups of six or less measurements, no lower control limit for the R chart is calculated.

For the $\overline{X}$ chart, the control limits are calculated as follows, using two more decimal places than the data points:

$$LCL_{\overline{x}} = \overline{X} - A_2 \, \overline{R}$$

$$UCL_{\overline{x}} = \overline{X} - A_2 \, \overline{R}$$

For the R chart, the corresponding formulae for the control limits are as follows, using one more decimal place than the individual measurements:

$$LCL_R = D_3 \, \overline{R}$$

$$LCL_R = D_3 \, \overline{R}$$

7. Draw the axes adding the right variable notations, Divide the axes into suitable intervals, and indicate any other relevant information (for example, when the measurement was performed, by whom, sample size). Draw the center line and control limits, using a solid line for the center line and dotted lines for the control limits.

The number of data points in the subgroup, n	Factors for the $\overline{X}$ chart, A_2	Factors for the lower control limit of the R chart, D_3	Factors for the upper control limit of the R chart, D_4
2	1.880	—	3.267
3	1.023	—	2.575
4	0.729	—	2.282
5	0.577	—	2.115
6	0.483	—	2.004
7	0.419	0.076	1.924
8	0.373	0.136	1.864
9	0.337	0.184	1.816
10	0.308	0.223	1.777

Table 10.1. Calculation factors.

8. Plot the data points as new measurements are made. Interpretation and actions are explained in the next subchapter.

Examples of these types of charts are shown in Figures 10.16 and 10.17.

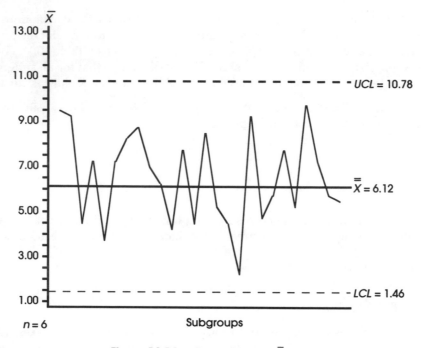

Figure 10.16.   Example of an $\bar{X}$ chart.

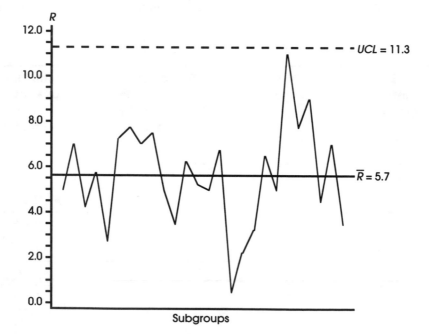

Figure 10.17.   Example of an R chart.

x and R Charts

As the title shows, this is also a pair of charts, used respectively for the centering and the variation. As previously mentioned, this is a less sensitive chart than the preceding one, but one that is useful where measurement is very expensive or difficult. The construction follows almost the same steps as for the $\overline{X}$ and R charts, only using slightly different calculation formulae for the control limits. The steps are thus as follows:

1. Collect the data, typically more than 25 measurements of recent date are required.

2. Calculate the mean value for the entire data set, $\overline{X}$. This value will represent the center line of x chart.

3. Calculate the ranges, R, for the data set, where R is defined as the numerical distance between one data point and the preceding one. Thus, for the first data point, no R is calculated, resulting in the number of R values being one less than the total number of measurements.

4. Calculate the average range, $\overline{R}$, for the entire data set by finding the mean of all the range values calculated in step 3. This value represents the center line of the R chart.

5. Calculate the control limits for both charts. To simplify the calculations, calculation factors have been developed that correspond to a deviation of $\pm$ three standard deviations. For the x chart, this factor is 2.66, which gives the following calculation formulae for the control limits of this chart:

$$LCL_x = \overline{X} - 2.66\overline{R}$$

$$UCL_x = \overline{X} + 2.66\overline{R}$$

For the R chart, we know that the sample size is always two, as the range is the distance between two measurements. Thus, we can use the factor $n = 2$ from Table 10.1. For the upper control limit, we see that the factor is 3.267, while we remember that for sample sizes of six or less, there is not a lower limit. The expression for the upper control limit is thus:

$$UCL_R = \overline{X} - 3.267\overline{R}$$

6. Draw the axes adding the right variable notations, divide the axes into suitable intervals, and indicate any other relevant information, for example, when the measurement was performed, by whom, sample size, and so on. Furthermore, draw the center line and control limits, using a solid line for the center line and dotted lines for the control limits.

7. Plot the data points as new measurements are made. Interpretation and actions are explained in the next subchapter.

The R chart will look exactly like the example in Figure 10.17, while the x chart will be very similar to the example in Figure 10.16, with a different variable name for the y axis. No separate examples for these two charts have therefore been included.

p *Chart*

Unlike the charts described this far, which are applied to variable data, the charts for attribute data are not used in pairs. Each chart for attribute data covers both the centering and the variation width. The procedure to construct a p chart, where p represents the portion of defective units, is as follows:

1. Collect the data set to be used for the construction of the chart and divide the measurements into subgroups sorted by date or series, for example. Generally, there should be more than 25 subgroups of a sample size, n, with 50 or more in each subgroup, and where the average number of defectives, np, is larger than three to four. The data set should come from a recently performed process run.

2. For each subgroup, the portion of defectives, p, is calculated simply by dividing the total number of defectives with the sample size, n, and multiplying by 100 to produce a percentage figure.

3. The center line of the chart is the average defective portion for the entire data set, $\bar{p}$, which is arrived at by dividing the total number of defectives by the total number of units inspected.

4. The control limits are calculated using the following formulae:

$$LCL_p = \bar{p} - 3\sqrt{\frac{\bar{p}(1 - \bar{p})}{n}}$$

$$LCL_p = \bar{p} + 3\sqrt{\frac{\bar{p}(1 - \bar{p})}{n}}$$

   If the numerical value for the lower control limit is negative, no lower limit can be calculated, so it is left out of the chart. Also notice that as the sample size, n, changes with time, the control limits also change. This means that for each subgroup of a different sample size, new control limits must be calculated. As this is very cumbersome, a simplification has been devised that does not give results that are too inaccurate. If all subgroups have a sample size that lies within ±20 percent of the average sample size, in the preceding formulae, the n of the denominators can be replaced by the average sample size, $\bar{n}$. For subgroups of sample sizes outside this 20 percent limit, separate limits must be calculated.

5. Draw the axes adding the right variable notations, divide the axes into suitable intervals, and indicate any other relevant information, for example, when the measurement was performed, by whom, sample size, and so on. Draw the center line and control limits, using a solid line for the center line and dotted lines for the control limits.

6. Plot the data points as new measurements are made. Interpretation and actions are explained in the next subchapter.

All four chart types for attribute data look like the preceding examples, using a different variable for the center line. Thus, no separate examples have been prepared.

np *Chart*

While the *p* chart can be used for samples of varying size, the *np* chart can only be used for samples of constant size. Otherwise, the procedure is quite similar to the one used for the *p* chart:

1. Collect the data set to be used for the construction of the chart and divide the measurements into subgroups. Generally, there should be more than 25 subgroups of a constant sample size, *n*, of 50 or more, with an average number of defectives, *np*, that is larger than three to four. The data set should come from a recently performed process run.

2. The center line of the chart is the average defective portion per subgroup, $n\bar{p}$, which is arrived at by dividing the total number of defective units by the number of subgroups.

3. The control limits are calculated using the following formulae:

$$LCL_{np} = n\bar{p} - 3\sqrt{n\bar{p}(1-\bar{p})}$$

$$UCL_{np} = n\bar{p} + 3\sqrt{n\bar{p}(1-\bar{p})}$$

If the numerical value for the lower control limit is negative, no lower limit can be calculated, and is therefore left out of the chart.

4. Draw the axes adding the right variable notations, divide the axes into suitable intervals, and indicate any other relevant information, for example, when the measurement was performed, by whom, sample size, and so on. Draw the center line and control limits, using a solid line for the center line and dotted lines for the control limits.

5. Plot the data points as new measurements are made. Interpretation and actions are explained in the next subchapter.

u *Chart*

As previously mentioned, the main difference between *p/np* charts and *u/c* charts is that the first are used for defective units, while the latter are used for the number of defects. Defects do not necessarily mean that the unit is defective. The *u* chart is used for samples of varying size, and is constructed according to the following steps:

1. Collect the data points. Typically, there should be more than 25 data pairs consisting of the number of units inspected, *n*, and the number of defects found, *c*. The data set should be recent and the number of inspected units should be higher than 50 with an average number of defects per subgroup of more than one to three.

2. For each subgroup, the portion of defects, *u*, is calculated (that is, the number of defects, *c*, is divided by the sample size, *n*). Because the sample size varies, this must be done for each subgroup.

3. The center line of the chart is the average defect portion, $\bar{u}$. This can be found by dividing the total number of defects in the entire data set by the total number of inspected units.

4. The control limits are calculated using the following formulae:

$$LCL_u = \bar{u} - 3\sqrt{\frac{u}{n}}$$

$$UCL_u = \bar{u} + 3\sqrt{\frac{u}{n}}$$

If the numerical value for the lower control limit is negative, no lower limit can be calculated, and it is left out of the chart. Please notice that as the sample size, $\bar{n}$, changes with time, the control limits also change. This means that for each subgroup of a different sample size, new control limits must be calculated. A similar simplification to the one used for the p chart can be used in this case. If all subgroups have a sample size that lies within ±20 percent of the average sample size, the n of the denominators can be replaced by the average sample size, n in the preceding formulae. For subgroups of sample sizes outside this 20 percent limit, separate limits must be calculated.

5. Draw the axes, adding the right variable notations, divide the axes into suitable intervals, and indicate any other relevant information, for example, when the measurement was performed, by whom, sample size, and so on. Draw the center line and control limits, using a solid line for the center line and dotted lines for the control limits.

6. Plot the data points as new measurements are made. Interpretation and actions are explained in the next subchapter.

c Chart

For the last chart type, the chart for portion of defects in samples of constant size, the procedure is quite similar to that used for the u chart:

1. Collect the data points and divide them into subgroups. Typically, there should be more than 25 subgroups of more than 50 recent measurements, with an average number of defects per subgroup of more than two to three.

2. The center line of the chart is the average number of defects, c. This can be found by dividing the total number of defects in the entire data set by the number of subgroups.

3. The control limits are calculated using the following formulae:

$$LCL_c = \bar{c} - 3\sqrt{\bar{c}}$$

$$UCL_c = \bar{c} + - 3\sqrt{\bar{c}}$$

If the numerical value for the lower control limit is negative, no lower limit can be calculated, and is therefore left out of the chart.

4. Draw the axes, adding the right variable notations, divide the axes into suitable intervals, and indicate any other relevant information, for example, when the measurement was performed, by whom, sample size, and so on. Furthermore, draw the center line and control limits, using a solid line for the center line and dotted lines for the control limits.

5. Plot the data points as new measurements are made. Interpretation and actions are explained in the next subchapter.

10.5.5 Interpreting the Control Charts

It is important to be able to select the right chart type for a given situation and able to construct that chart. The chart is only useful when we are able to interpret the meaning of the data points and understand what actions should be undertaken.

Most of the variation seen in a control chart is chronic variation, which is a natural part of the process. This variation requires no adjustments or tampering with the process to keep it under control. However, it should be a constant objective to improve the process, that is, improve the expected value and/or reduce the natural variation width. If the process for issuing an important document is stabilized at an expected value of three hours and twenty minutes and a standard deviation of thirty minutes, SPC can very well be used for registering that after some time, it has been improved to an average of two hours and a standard deviation of fifteen minutes.

Only a small portion of the variation can be attributed to special causes, what we called sporadic variation, which require special attention or action. Results that fall outside the control limits obviously constitute such variation, as do patterns of variation within the limits, which can signal the existence of special causes. In the following, some examples of control charts displaying different types of variation and the meaning of these are presented.

1. The natural progression of a process under control that only displays variation that can be statistically expected, is shown in the previous examples (see for instance, Figure 10.16). Unless there is a wish to improve such a process, there is no need to anything about it.

2. Figure 10.18 shows a control chart in which one point has fallen outside the upper control limit. It is statistically very improbable that this should happen, with limits based on three times the standard deviation, only two or three of 1000 will fall outside. There is, however, sufficient probability that one isolated point, a so-called wild card, can exist without it being possible to find any special cause for it. If no more points appear outside the limits in a short time, this is not alarming.

3. If several points fall outside the limits, as shown in Figure 10.19, they can hardly be explained in any other way than being the results of special causes. A search for the causes must then be started in order to eliminate them, thus preventing a reoccurrence.

4. A process is changing or is unstable if either two of three consecutive points on the same side of the center line are more than two standard deviations away from it, or four of five consecutive points on the same side of the center line are more than one standard deviation away from it. One example is shown in Figure 10.20. Such a change in level indicates a special cause, for

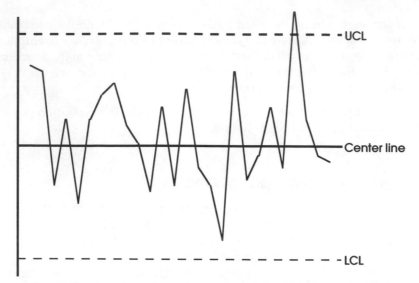

Figure 10.18. Control chart with one point outside the control limits.

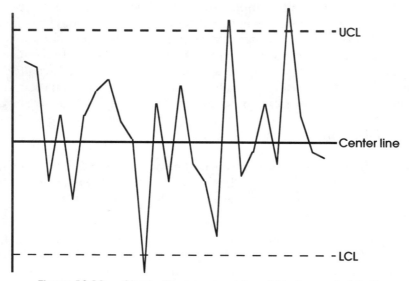

Figure 10.19. Chart with several points outside the control limits.

example that a new operator has taken over, a new material has been introduced, a new tool has been put to use, and so on. If the cause is found, new control limits must be calculated under the new conditions before the monitoring is continued. Incidentally, if this is due to a change in operators, this is a good opportunity for improving the process. The operator producing the best results can teach the other what he is doing, that is, some form of benchmarking between operators.

5. Another sign indicating that the centering of the process has been changed, is if relatively many points fall on the same side of the center line. Initially, we would expect equally many points on either side of the center line. If series of seven, 10 of 11, 12 of 14, or 14 of 17 fall on the same side, this indicates sys-

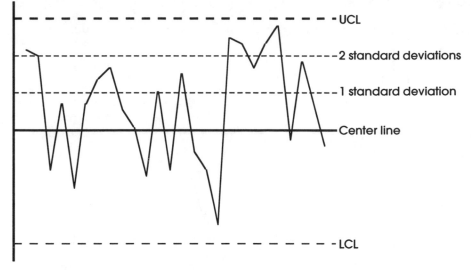

Figure 10.20.   Process with change in level.

tematic variation. The causes for the change must be found and eliminated. An example is shown Figure 10.21.

6. Furthermore, we expect that the measurements would alternately increase and decrease from the previous measurement. A trend where six or more measurements show constant increase or decrease, as shown in Figure 10.22, is a signal that the process is changing. Again, the causes must be found and counteracted.

7. While at the same time alternating measurements should be expected on both sides of the center line, it is statistically improbable that fourteen or more points should systematically alternate from one side to the other. This is shown in Figure 10.23, and is probably caused by tampering with the process, that is, continuously changing the centering based on individual measurements.

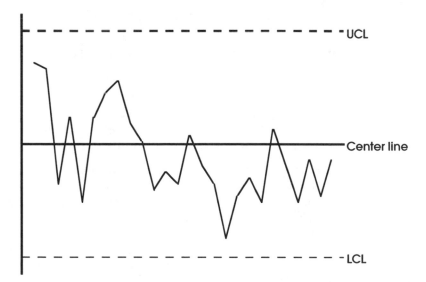

Figure 10.21.   A series of 12 of 14 points on the same side of the center line.

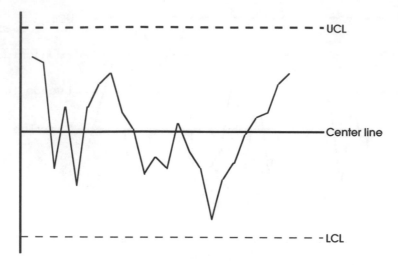

Figure 10.22.   Process with trend.

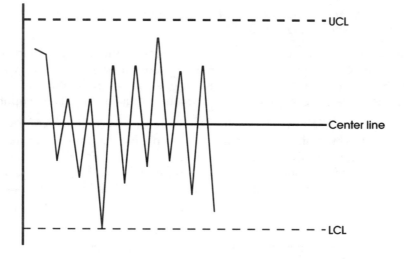

Figure 10.23.   Process that is probably being tampered with.

8. The last alternative when it comes to the appearance of the control chart is shown in Figure 10.24. Here, it is possible to see clear cycles of the measurements, which is probably caused by rotation of operators, a process spanning several shifts, temperature changes throughout the day, and so on.

When using statistical process control, we must combine a basic understanding of the process being monitored with good knowledge about the appearance of the control charts. This way, SPC is a powerful tool that can be used both for inspecting the process and for improving it. It is important that signals from the chart that indicate that something is wrong must be followed up quickly. It is quite common in companies using SPC that when the operator is not immediately able to determine special causes, a cross-functional team is established to continue working on the case. Such groups are treated in chapter 11.

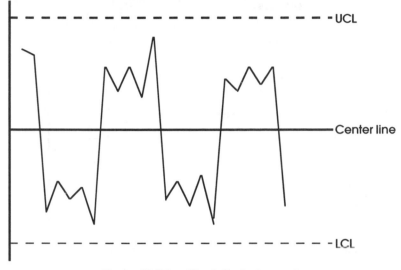

Figure 10.24.   Chart displaying cycles.

10.5.6 Process Capability

As it is connected to the treatment of statistical process, it is logical to cover the concept of process capability. This concept is used to determine whether a process, given its natural variation, is capable of satisfying the specifications. A process can very well be under statistical control and still not be able to produce units or results that satisfy the specifications. When calculating the process capability, an index is used to compare the specifications with the control limits.

Specifications normally define a nominal value, the desired result, plus/minus a value saying something about how large a deviation from the desired value can be accepted without negatively impacting the functionality. Normally, two-sided tolerance limits are specified (that is, both an upper and lower limit, UTL and LTL), while for some processes, only one of the limits is specified.

The least complex of two capability indexes, Cp compares the difference between the tolerance limits with the natural variation of the process. If the distance between the tolerance limits exceeds six times the standard deviation, the process can stay within the specification, provided it has been centered on the nominal value. The index is calculated as follows:

$$Cp = \frac{UTL - LTL}{6\sigma}$$

The standard deviation, σ, for the process is rarely known, and must therefore be estimated. This is done by calculating the average range, that is, the difference between the highest and the lowest value within a subgroup, for all subgroups. This is usually R. Then, an estimation of the standard deviation is calculated using the following formula:

$$\sigma = \frac{\overline{R}}{d_2}$$

The factor d_2 has already been calculated and can be found in Table 10.2, depending on the sample size, n.

Sample size, n	d_2
2	1.128
3	1.693
4	2.059
5	2.326
6	2.534
7	2.704
8	2.847
9	2.970
10	3.078

Table 10.2.   Factors for estimating the standard deviation.

A general rule for this simple index is that it should be greater than 1.2 or more. This ensures that the process variation is sufficiently small compared to the specifications. The problem with this index however, is, that it does not capture the fact that the process can be unevenly centered compared to the nominal value. It is of little help if the variation is small compared to the tolerance limits, that is, if the center of it is located close to one of the limits.

Therefore, a less sensitive index has been introduced, termed C_{pk}. This index both covers the variation of the process as well the centering of it. It actually consists of two indexes, one lower and one upper, C_{pl} and C_{pu}. The smallest of these is used as C_{pk}. They are calculated as follows:

$$C_{pl} = \frac{\overline{\overline{X}}\ LTL}{3\sigma}$$

$$C_{pu} = \frac{UTL - \overline{\overline{X}}}{3\sigma}$$

$\overline{\overline{X}}$ in this case means the average value for the process. Values below 1.0 mean that a 100 percent inspection must be performed. If any changes in the process's centering can be accepted, C_{pk} must be greater than 1.33, while it should be 2.0 or even larger. The ideal is that the index is over 5.0. This index can be used to determine whether the existing process is at all able to produce what is required, to realistic tolerance limits suited to the process, and to negotiate targets for suppliers' process capability.

A manufacturer of various types of special cables experienced high quantities of cables with defects. In fact, defects were so common that producing excess quantities to cover up for this had become the norm. All of this happened in spite of the fact that stringent inspection had been installed along the entire manufacturing line. Each single operator was responsible for undertaking visual control of the cable they were working on.

To investigate what caused the defects and possibly correct them, the company wanted to try statistical process control. First, one day's production was viewed as a sample. Since a cable with defects in practice always was defective and had to be scrapped, a chart type covering defectives was

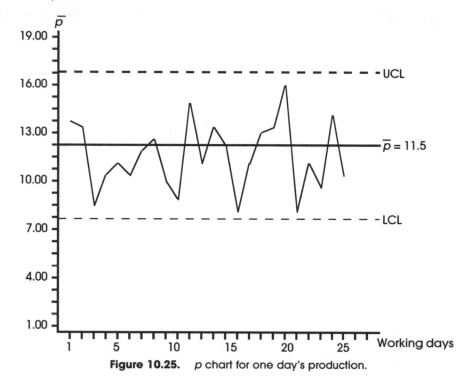

Figure 10.25. *p* chart for one day's production.

selected. A *p* chart based on data for the entire preceding month was first constructed. The center line was calculated at an average defective portion of 11.5 percent, which gave the chart shown in Figure 10.25.

As the chart shows, the process was actually under control, with an average portion of defectives of 11.5 percent. This was shocking news that revealed how large a portion of defectives the company generated. To learn why the process was performing so poorly, the data points were divided into other subgroups. Instead of viewing the entire day's production as one, data was collected representing a week's production from each individual operator. A new *p* chart, as shown in Figure 10.26, was constructed.

This chart quite clearly revealed that while the other operators generated few defectives, operator number 5 and 12 were at the other end of the scale. After having studied these two more closely, the explanation was found. Both had such poor eyesight that they did not discover the many smaller defects that caused defective units. The company covered the costs for glasses for them, which quickly gave results. The average portion of defectives was continuously reduced and after three months was down to 1.85 percent. This number was still too high, but significantly better than the starting point. After this, the differences between the operators were so small that common charts could be used for the entire production of a day.

10.6 Business Process Reengineering

Business process reengineering, commonly abbreviated BPR, is a concept that is becoming more and more widespread and should probably be viewed as the fashion tool of

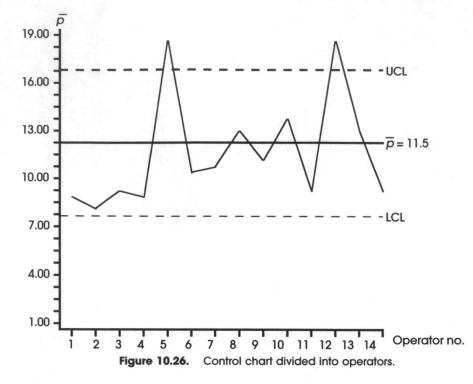

Figure 10.26. Control chart divided into operators.

the 1990s, perhaps second only to benchmarking (see next subchapter). The history of BPR is not very clear, but its roots are most likely found in the United States. As have other popular tools, BPR has been defined in a number of more or less different ways. According to Hammer and Champy (1993), BPR is:

> *Reengineering is fundamental rethinking and radical redesign of business processes to achieve dramatic improvements in critical contemporary measures of performance, such as cost, quality, service, and speed.*

This definition focuses on the objectives of BPR, that is, the so-called break-through improvements. This element is also present in a definition by Peppard and Rowland (1995):

> *BPR is an improvement philosophy. It aims to achieve step improvements in performance by redesigning the processes through which an organization operates, maximizing their value-added content and minimizing everything else. This approach can be applied at an individual process level or to the whole organization.*

Comparing these two definitions with some of the other tools available, many differences are apparent, but also some similarities. What primarily separates BPR from the tools presented so far is the strong emphasis on the breakthroughs or radical improvements. BPR is not the tool to select if the objective it to achieve a 10 percent improvement. It is rather a strategic tool that can be useful when the organization wishes to achieve dramatic improvements in its performance level. At the same time, this seems very close to the streamlining presented in an earlier chapter, that is, increasing the proportion of value-adding activities in the processes. The fact is, BPR is a collection of more or less related tools. Unlike streamlining, they have been put together to form a structured process that, when coherently applied, can generate the desired breakthrough improvement.

It is not the intention of this book to dwell on definitions of BPR. It should, however, be mentioned that there are two principally different approaches when it comes to how BPR is carried out. These two approaches are linked to the role existing business processes play when applying BPR:

- Should the existing processes form the basis for the new, redesigned processes?

- Should the existing processes be changed in the improvement phase, or should new processes be designed to replace them?

- Should the organization simply start the reengineering with a clean sheet?

So far in this book, much emphasis has been put on understanding our existing business processes. Ignoring these processes is very risky, as it means ignoring the knowledge and experience that have been accumulated over a long period of time. In addition, there is a risk of repeating the same mistakes. It is also a fact that very few organizations have succeeded in implementing completely new processes. On the other hand, it avoids the danger of becoming buried in too many details of the existing processes, and therefore allowing the limitations incorporated in them to impact the new process, and thus limit improvement. As for most matters in this area, there are no correct answers. Between extremes, there are an endless number of degrees to which the existing processes influence the BPR effort. The important issue is to strike a suitable balance between how things are done today and how they should be done in a perfect world.

Based on two extremes, two types of BPR can be defined:

- Systematic reengineering, where the current processes are understood, documented, and analyzed in order to systematically create new and better processes.

- Clean sheet reengineering, where the current processes are scrapped and new processes created from scratch through fundamental rethinking.

The first of these, systematic reengineering, can in many cases be synonymous with streamlining. Because starting with completely a clean sheet rarely can be done in practice, when referring to BPR throughout this book, something more moderate is intended. As opposed to streamlining, BPR is not only about incremental improvements in existing processes. BPR must seek to combine the best from existing processes with new ideas about how the ideal process should look. This is quite close to the technique of, whose objective was to create an image of the ideal process. Thus, a true application of BPR will be a structured process where these two elements, idealizing and streamlining, are combined.

Let us now leave the definition area and devote the rest of the description of BPR to how to apply it. A process for conducting a BPR project will be described.

10.6.1 A Process for Conducting Business Process Reengineering

There are many alternative processes that describe a BPR project. The process presented in this book is inspired by Kubeck (1995). As with most other improvement processes, this process can be divided into a planning part, a solutions generation part, and an implementation part. Since, by definition, the solutions generated in BPR can deviate radically from the existing processes, the middle stage has been divided into two phases, one for the actual generation of change proposals and one to evaluate how these can be implemented. This gives a process spanning four phases, as depicted in Figure 10.27.

1. *Planning*, where the focus for the BPR project is selected, a team to carry out the project is formed, and, if possible, objectives for the project are defined.

2. *Reengineering*, where, more or less based on the existing process, a set of techniques is employed to reengineer the process to a level that will result in significant improvements.

3. *Transformation*, where it is determined how the reengineered process can be implemented, both with regard to the existing process, the need for investments, training, and so on.

4. *Implementation*, where the solutions generated and approved during the two preceding phases are implemented and the process changed.

10.6.2 Planning

The central tasks in this phase are:

- Select the process to be improved through BPR and consider its scope.

- Assess the possibilities for achieving improvements and establish targets.

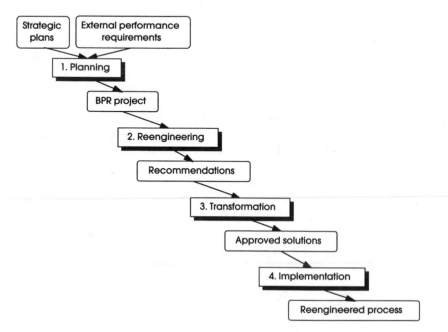

Figure 10.27. The process for conducting a BPR project.

- Establish a project team to perform the work in the project.

- Produce a project plan for the BPR project.

If this were a book dealing exclusively with BPR, the planning phase would have been described using several pages. However, if the content of this phase is related to what has already been treated in this book, most of the tasks have already been discussed and performed in the overall improvement process. The first step, selecting the process to be improved, is based on the results from the improvement planning of chapter 5. Based on an assessment of the current performance level, external performance requirements, and the organization's strategic plans, a prioritization was made of business processes or areas in need of improvement. Starting from this prioritized list, the BPR project will normally start at a point in time where the process to improve has already been selected.

The next step is an introductory assessment of whether BPR really is a suitable tool for improving this process. It is necessary to consider which improvement targets are realistic and desirable. This will aid in securing the necessary resources, both time and money, that are alloted for the project.

The next task of the planning phase is to establish a project team. Most of the tools presented in this book are meant for use in teams or groups of some form. Some general guidelines for forming such groups were outlined in chapter 2.

The last step in this phase is producing a project plan. The need for a project plan obviously exists when using any of the previously presented tools, but since BPR normally results in a more extensive project than the others, project planning has not been described before. Just as few people would start a long journey without a roadmap and a planned route or start building a house without a blueprint, such a project should not be started without a project plan. The plan need not result from hours of intense planning, it should simply represent some form of route through the landscape toward an implemented improvement. Some central points that should be included in the plan are:

- Activities of the project.

- Who will perform these?

- When they should be performed?

- Which resources are needed and which are available for the project.

- The expected results from the project.

Depending on the scope and complexity of the project, the project plan can be made as detailed as necessary. The project plan should not be a strait jacket, but rather a guideline for the ensuing work. Should a better route or a short-cut be discovered, it is perfectly acceptable to deviate from the original route.

One last remark about the planning phase of the BPR project: the preceding description actually fits any preparation phase regardless of what tool is being used. This description is not unique to BPR, but can be used in any improvement project. The BPR-specific content appears in the next phase, the reengineering phase.

10.6.3 Reengineering

The main purpose of this phase is, as the name implies, to reengineer the process to be improved. Before and after this main task, there is preparation and tidying up to do, thus the steps of this phase are:

- Document the existing process
- Reengineer the process
- Develop recommendations for improvement

Whether choosing one or the other extreme when it comes to BPR approach (that is, systematic reengineering or clean sheet) there is a need to know how the process is currently carried out. The first step of this phase is therefore to document the current process, usually by using a flowchart. If the general structure of the book and its approach to improvement work has been followed, this job has already been done. This simplifies the work in this phase and renders it possible to start with the reengineering task. If much time has passed since the process was documented or if those participating in the BPR team are not familiar with this documentation, it might be necessary to update or repeat it. Process, by the way, is treated in chapter 3.

Turning to the reengineering of the business process itself, the procedure is dependent on the extent to which it is based on the existing process. Therefore, the two procedures are described separately.

Systematic Reengineering

As has been mentioned, this resembles the streamlining described in chapter 10.1. In BPR literature, the so-called ESIA rules are often referred to. They are rules and techniques designed to accomplish four core steps in the systematic of an existing process.

- Elimination
- Simplification

Eliminate	Simplify	Integrate	Automate
Excess production	Forms	Jobs	Dirty work
Waiting time	Procedures	Groups	Difficult work
Transport	Communication	Customers	Dangerous work
Processing	Technology	Suppliers	Boring work
Storage	Problem areas		Data capturing
Defects/errors	Flow		Data transfer
Duplication	Processes		Data analysis
Reformatting			
Inspection			
Reconsolidation			

Table 10.3. Focus areas for systematic reengineering.

Peppard, Joe, and Philip Rowland. *The Essence of Business Process Reengineering.* Prentice Hall, Hemel Hempstead, England, 1995. Used by permission.

- Integration

- Automation

The main areas where each of these can be applied are listed Table 10.3 (Peppard and Rowland, 1995).

The ESIA rules should be applied in this order. The first step is to eliminate all activities that do not add value (see also chapter 10.1). In organizations where process thinking is novel, a number of activities usually turn out to be non value-adding and thus eligible for elimination without any negative consequences. Toyota uses as a rule-of-thumb that in many of the traditional manufacturing processes, at any point in time, 85 percent of the employees will be performing non-productive work (Griffiths, 1993):

- 5 percent can be observed not working

- 25 percent are waiting for something

- 30 percent are manufacturing something that increases inventory levels, which is not value-adding

- 25 percent are working, but in accordance with less efficient standards or procedures

It is thus obvious that dramatic improvements can be achieved by attacking the areas listed under the heading of elimination in Table 10.3 and, of course, truly managing to eliminate them.

When as many as possible of these unnecessary tasks have been eliminated, the next step is to simplify as many of those remaining as possible. Areas that are often overly complex, are where the elements listed under Simplification Table 10.3 are generally involved

Thereafter, the remaining tasks are to integrate and further improve the flow of deliveries between the suppliers, the organization, and the customers. This can be accomplished at several levels. First of all, several smaller jobs can often be integrated into one single job. Such a job extension has several positive effects, it both enriches the content of the individual employee's work while at the same time eliminates interfacing between areas of responsibility. All such interfaces, no matter how well managed, create waiting time and potential quality problems. Furthermore, different individual specialists can be integrated into groups that are responsible for more jobs. The closeness and autonomy created result in many of the same positive effects as the integration of several jobs into one. The third level is to attempt integrating the organization with customers and suppliers. The organizations that achieve a particularly close relationship to their suppliers and customers usually experience more stable conditions and display better opportunities for common improvement. A typical application is to integrate suppliers of core components and customers into the product development processes.

The final approach is automation. Information technology, computerization, and robotic equipment are support aids that can be quite powerful and give very good results, if the processes being automated from the outset are sound. Automating problem processes can in many cases make things worse, that is, automation can enable errors to be made more rapidly. Therefore, it is essential to apply the principle of automation last, after elimination, simplification, and integration have been successfully applied. Processes suitable for automation are also listed in Table 10.3.

Automation usually fits the 80/20 rule. While many automation projects strive for 100 percent functionality in the automated system, a general rule is that 80 percent functionality can be achieved at 20 percent of the cost. Making systems that take into account every possible exception and special case can be very expensive. If a system that can handle most cases, with occasional manual intervention is acceptable, both time and money can be saved.

Clean Sheet

It is difficult to give general advice about how to proceed with the clean sheet approach, that is, starting with a clean sheet and drawing an entirely new process. There are few, if any, specific techniques for this objective; we are instead dependent on creativity, imagination, knowledge about available technology and human resources, and so on. Each BPR project utilizing this approach is unique. Some basic questions that need answering, however, are:

- *Which* basic needs do we want to fulfill, and for whom? By answering this question, we might realize that there are services or products that are preferable to those currently provided. A manufacturer of explosives asked this question, and the answer was that the need it was fulfilling was the need for a hole in a rock, not the explosives per se. The customers would prefer to have the hole supplied without using the explosives. The company started offering its services as explosive experts in addition to marketing the explosives themselves, delivering finished holes at the points indicated by the customers.

- *Why* do we try to fulfill these needs? Does it fit in with the overall strategy of the organization?

- *Where* must these needs be fulfilled? At home, in a separate service area, in the company's facilities? The answer to this question can also form the basis for dramatic changes in the processes. This happened in the restaurant industry, which discovered that not all customers wanted to have their needs fulfilled in a restaurant, but also in their own homes. Thus, express deliveries of warm food to private homes were created.

- *When* must these needs be fulfilled? At what time of the day, and by which deadlines? Even if this is not a pure BPR project, many service institutions such as stores and banks, have adapted their operating hours to meet the customers' needs. This entailed many changes in their processes to accommodate afternoon or evening needs fulfillment.

- *How* will the needs be fulfilled? What processes will be required? Who must perform these processes, and which technologies does this require? After having answered all of these basic questions, we should start thinking about practical issues regarding how to accomplish this. This way, these basic questions are not clouded by practical limitations.

Just by looking at these questions and the basic challenge the approach of clean sheets poses, it is obvious that the creativity of the persons involved is crucial. Some further questions to inspire the necessary creativity and imagination are:

- If you were to create a competitor of your own organization, how should it look to have the highest possible impact?

- How should the ideal process look?

- If we could build the entire organization from scratch, how would the organization and this specific process look?

These questions are summarized in Figure 10.28. Crazy ideas stemming from brainstorming not limited by practical considerations are combined with the answers to the preceding questions, ideas from benchmarking of other processes (benchmarking is described in chapter 10), available human resources, and technological opportunities.

The last issue in the reengineering phase, no matter which approach has been used, is to summarize what changes are needed to implement the new process. By comparing on paper the newly designed process to the old process, we can decide which changes are required. This list of recommended changes will form the basis for the work in the next phase, the transformation phase.

10.6.4 Transformation

The main purpose of this phase is to build the foundation for an effective and successful implementation of the new process. The main tasks will be:

- Evaluating the changes required to implement the new process

- Planning the need for investments, training, purchases, and so on

- Creating a favorable climate for change

- Planning the implementation

The reengineering phase created a number of recommendations for change, without critically assessing their feasibility. The first step of the transformation phase is to apply a more sober perspective on things so as to evaluate whether all activities are possible to implement. The purpose is, of course, not to be so critical that most of the recommendations are rejected, but rather to ensure that infeasible changes or changes in opposition to the organization's strategy are removed. For example, a recommendation that the company change its operating hours from 9 A.M. to 5 P.M. to 2 P.M. to 11 P.M., might be so radically against the human resource policy that it should be rejected.

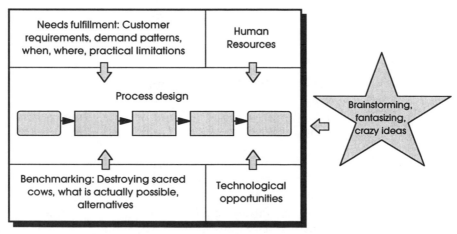

Figure 10.28.   Process design from a clean sheet.

The next issue is to map the need for the changes and plan the necessary investments, training, new staff, and so on. Many of the recommended changes will require these kinds of efforts, and the needs must be known in advance of the planning of the implementation itself. If not, we risk, for instance, introducing the new process to operators who have not been sufficiently trained, as this requirement was never identified.

Before the actual implementation starts, it is very important that the right climate for change be created. Even the best most well-planned improvement projects can be sabotaged if those who are impacted by the changes do not support them. Creating such a favorable climate is a science of its own, one that is not covered by this book. A general and basic condition that always contributes a positively, is to have those who will later have to live with the changes take part in planning them. This means that including in the project team persons already deeply involved in the process will create a good foundation for a painless implementation. Another issue is to always be open and honest about what is in the pipeline and provide a continuous flow of information to the affected parties. A department facing extensive change is like an area of low pressure in the atmosphere. It will suck up information of any sort until it is filled up. If this information is not constructive information from the management, it will be rumors and gossip that can be harmful to the situation. Force field analysis, as treated in chapter 12, is a suitable tool for creating the desired climate.

The last step before the implementation phase is planning. The need for this plan is very similar to the need for a plan for the BPR project itself, and must contain approximately the same elements, in addition to the required investments, training, and so on.

10.6.5 Implementation

Like the planning phase, this phase of the BPR project, where changes are effected, is quite general. Regardless of which improvement project is being discussed, the last activity will always be implementation of improvements. Beyond the fact that the changes resulting from a BPR project often are more comprehensive than when other tools are used, this phase in the BPR project is not in any way unique. At the same time, there is no doubt that the implementation can be the most difficult phase. Many improvement projects that have performed excellently to this point fail in implementation.

At this point in the book, the implementation phase will not be described in any detail, but rather be described more generally in chapter 12. However, coarsely, the steps of this phase will look as follows:

- Set targets for the improvements.

- Carry out the implementation plan.

- Monitor the progress of the implementation and handle any deviations.

Finally, many talk about the two tools of BPR and benchmarking simultaneously, and they are to some extent related. This is treated in the next subchapter.

As an example of the use of BPR, we will look at a manufacturer of hydraulic hoisting equipment for industrial applications. This company produced some standard systems, accounting for about 60 percent of the sales. At the same time, the company offered tailor-made solutions for all potential purposes. Their reputation in the market was that they could do almost any-thing. Thus, for almost half of the sales, some degree of redesign of stan-dard systems or development of new products and engineer new solutions was required.

The company was one of very few in the market offering tailor-made systems, but lately, several competitors had moved into this segment. Some competitors could offer shorter delivery times, even when the delivery involved product development, which endangered the competitiveness of our company. It was therefore decided to undertake a BPR project with the objective of reducing the delivery times for such systems by 50 percent.

Planning

The process to be improved was thus identified. A project team was estab-lished consisting of two persons from each of the following departments:

- Sales
- Manufacturing
- Product development (projects consisting of hydraulic and mechan-ical design)
- Procurement

The team decided to make a project plan, expecting a six months duration. The clean sheet approach was selected with consideration to the current sit-uation. Thus, the intention was to combine the best from the existing process with elements of the ideal process.

Reengineering

After having completed these introductory tasks, the next step was to doc-ument the current process, as shown in Figure 10.29.

A common denominator for the entire process was sequential develop-ment. First, the hydraulic department designed the core system functional-ity. Next, the mechanical department designed the mechanical system to fit the hydraulic system. Then the manufacturing department had to find a way to manufacture this system, while the procurement department was left to quarrel with the suppliers about components and processes for these. Often, the final product delivered to the customer was different from what the cus-tomer had actually tried to specify. On the positive side, a very rational process was used by the product development department to make draw-ings, system charts, bill-of-materials, and so on.

The core task of the BPR project, which was viewed with great expecta-tions, was to describe the ideal process. This task was carefully planned by:

- Involving people who were known for their creativity and enthusi-asm at work.
- Reserving two days per week for four weeks exclusively for this task.
- Creating in advance a climate of trust and cooperation within the group through two social gatherings.
- Ensuring the availability of all necessary aids for the job.

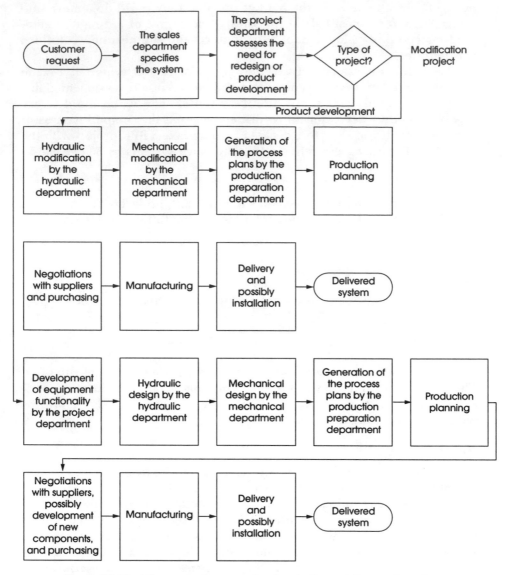

Figure 10.29.   The current process for developing a tailor-made system.

Without describing the group's work in detail, the result was an outline of an ideal process that all agreed represented a dramatic improvement over the current situation. The ideal process is depicted in Figure 10.30.

In this process, parallelism was emphasized, based on ideas from concurrent engineering, and cooperation between internal departments and external elements like the customers and suppliers. The project group found this ideal process to be so powerful that they wanted to implement as much of it as possible. The reengineering phase was therefore concluded by systematically summarizing all changes required to reach this target.

Transformation

As the transformation phase was started by employing a more sober attitude, talks with the customers and suppliers revealed that while most of them were

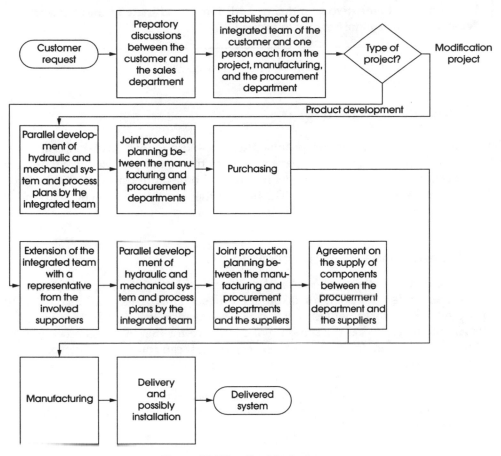

Figure 10.30.   The ideal process.

interested in cooperation, three central suppliers did not want this solution. Thus the involvment of suppliers in the integrated team was scrapped. No other obstacles were found against organizing such projects using integrated teams. No investments were required, but training was necessary in the areas of cooperation, group processes, and effective communication.

As central persons from the affected departments had participated in outlining the new process, the climate for change was from the outset favorable. To reinforce this climate, two one-day information seminars were planned where the project group, in cooperation with external resource persons within concurrent engineering, would present the project and its advantages. Also, an illustrating work group on the use of concurrent engineering was planned. An implementation plan was also produced during this seminar.

Implementation

The implementation of the new process took nine months longer than expected. The results, however, were well worth the effort. The average time from when the first customer request was received to when a complete system had been developed, manufactured, and delivered was reduced from

4.5 months to below two months. In addition, the climate in and between departments was significantly improved.

10.7 Benchmarking

Benchmarking has been mentioned numerous times throughout this book, usually as a tool whose core element is comparison. Before the actual process for conducting benchmarking is introduced, some definitions and other introductory issues related to benchmarking will be presented. The bulk of the description of benchmarking is based on Andersen and Pettersen (1996).

10.7.1 Definitions of Benchmarking

Looking exclusively at the noun *benchmarking*, its original meaning is a predefined position, used as a reference point for taking measures against. This word has migrated into the business world, where it has come to mean: a measured "best-in-class" achievement recognized as the standard of excellence for that business process.

Turning to the verb, or the activity, *benchmarking*, it can somewhat philosophically be defined as follows:

> *Benchmarking is the practice of being humble enough to admit that someone else is better at something, and being wise enough to learn how to match them and even surpass them at it (APQC, 1993).*

This definition captures the essence of benchmarking, namely learning from others. The term benchmark probably comes from geographic surveying, where points in the terrain are given with reference to a fixed point, often a tall peak or some other

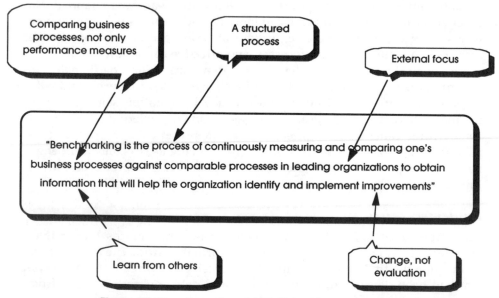

Figure 10.31.   Operational definition of benchmarking.

easily recognizable and definable point. At that point, two stone slates were raised on end and spaced somewhat apart and a third slate laid on top of these, thus forming a stone bench, hence the word benchmark. Based on its meaning of comparison against a reference point or the optimal, it was put to use in the business world, extended, and is currently defined as shown in Figure 10.31.

Many view benchmarking as a method for comparing key figures, often financial key figures, for the purpose of ranking the organization in relation to competitors or the industry average. This might have been the main application of benchmarking earlier, but today it is a far more powerful tool that is much more widely applicable. The core of the current interpretation of benchmarking is:

- *Measurement*, of your own and the benchmarking partners' performance level, both for comparison and for registering improvements.

- *Comparison*, of performance levels, processes, practices, and so on.

- *Learning*, from the benchmarking partners to introduce improvements in your own organization.

- *Improvement*, which is the ultimate objective of any benchmarking study.

Four main reasons for advocating the use of benchmarking in an organization that is striving to improve are:

1. Benchmarking helps the organization understand and develop a critical attitude toward its business processes.

2. Benchmarking encourages an active learning process in the organization and motivates change and improvement.

3. Through benchmarking, the organization can find new sources for improvement and new ways of doing things outside its own environment.

4. Through benchmarking, reference points are established for performance measurement of business processes.

Benchmarking is thus about comparison of your own organization against other organizations. Different types of benchmarking can be defined based on whom is being compared against and what is being compared.

Comparing against *whom*:

- *Internal benchmarking*—comparison against the best within the same organization or corporation, often called benchmarking within your own class.

- *Competitive benchmarking*—comparison against the best direct competitors, which then can be termed benchmarking against someone in a parallel class.

- *Functional benchmarking*—comparison against organizations that are not necessarily competitors, but that perform related tasks within the same technological area. In the school analogy, this will be benchmarking against someone from another school of the same type.

- *Generic benchmarking*—comparison against the best, regardless of industry or markets, which can be said to be benchmarking against someone from a totally different school.

Comparing these types of benchmarking, the further down the list we go, the further away from our own little world we move. This is illustrated in Figure 10.32. Comparing *what*:

- *Performance benchmarking*—comparison of pure key figures or other performance measures. If drawing a parallel to the world of sports, performance benchmarking says something about how high we should aim, but nothing about how to make that height.

- *Process benchmarking*—beyond performance measures, comparison of how business processes are performed, not only how well they are performed. This answers questions like how to jump, which equipment to use, and so on to clear this height.

- *Strategic benchmarking*—comparison of strategic decisions and dispositions at a higher level. This is a less frequently used variant of benchmarking. In the sports example, this could say something about which jumping field to select.

The differences are illustrated in Figure 10.33.

Each type from these two categories—that is, whom and what is being benchmarked—can in theory be combined into a benchmarking study with a given focus. In practice, not all of the possible combinations are equally suitable, as is shown in Figure 10.34. It will not be explained in detail, but different studies have shown that the best results are generally achieved by a combination of process benchmarking and generic benchmarking using partners from other industries.

The different types of benchmarking can be used in combination to some extent. A typical benchmarking study is outlined in Figure 10.35. Both to give an indication

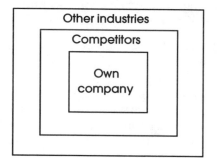

Figure 10.32. Benchmarking out of the box.

Figure 10.33. Three types of benchmarking based on what is being compared.

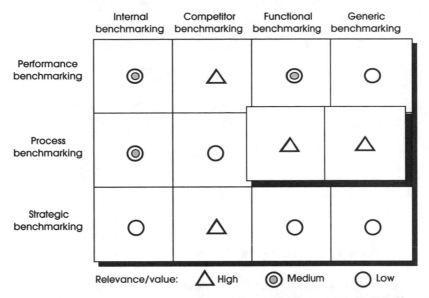

Figure 10.34.   Recommended combinations of types of benchmarking.

of where the organization stands and what should be improved, as well as finding possible benchmarking partners, as a start, performance benchmarking can be used. This was also mentioned during the description of performance planning in chapter 5. Next, process benchmarking is used to really improve through observing what the best do.

The last definition is that there are several models for how benchmarking can be conducted with respect to the relationship to others. The most common models are shown in Figure 10.36. The most used model is where one organization initiates a benchmarking study with several other organizations as benchmarking partners. A one-on-one comparison is made against each of these, often without letting the other partners know that more than one is being used, or who the others are.

Lately, it has become common practice for several organizations to join together to conduct a benchmarking study, where comparisons are made among all the organizations involved. This usually give better value for all partners involved.

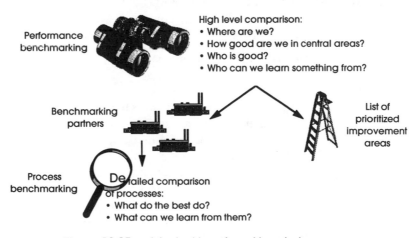

Figure 10.35.   A typical benchmarking study progress.

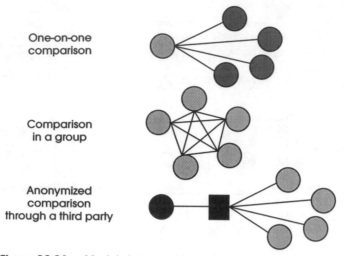

One-on-one
comparison

Comparison
in a group

Anonymized
comparison
through a third party

Figure 10.36.   Models for organizing a benchmarking study.

The third model, which is perhaps somewhat old-fashioned, is where a third party, usually a consultant, performs the data collection and analysis, and then presents the results to the organization who contributed their data. As each organization cannot observe the best practices in use, it is often difficult to make any changes based on such studies. The model is best suited for performance benchmarking.

10.7.2 Ethical and Legal Aspects of Benchmarking

In an early phase in the development of benchmarking, many critics voiced concern about its ethics. Many claimed that benchmarking was about getting as much information as possible from the benchmarking partners, without giving anything in return. This is of course not right, any benchmarking cooperation is based on mutual benefit. Still, it was accepted by the pioneers of benchmarking that it might be positioned somewhere on the borderline of the ethically acceptable, and several interest organizations for benchmarking teamed up to establish a set of ethical guidelines for benchmarking. These guidelines describe in detail how a benchmarking organization should behave in different situations. It will take too long to recite all the paragraphs here, but when compressed they turn out to be rather biblical:

- Do to your benchmarking partners as you want them to do to you.

- If you are in doubt whether an activity is legal or ethically justifiable, refrain from it.

It has at times been alleged that benchmarking is nothing but systemized industrial espionage. This is not true either, but at the same time, you should be aware of existing legislation that could limit the use of benchmarking. While no current U.S. legislation poses any difficulties for benchmarking organizations, the same might not be completely true in Europe. Article 85 of the European Treaty prohibits any agreement or conduct coordinated with others that can distort competition or have an effect on trade within the European market. Reading this article to the letter, it is easy to understand why some express concern with regard to benchmarking. Benchmarking is nothing if not conduct coordinated with others for the purpose of improvement, which in turn can distort competitive conditions. On the other hand, there have been few if any legal disputes on the use of benchmarking.

Either way, it might be pertinent to display some caution, especially when benchmarking using suppliers, customers, or competitors as benchmarking partners. In the latter case, under no circumstances should the benchmarking study focus on issues like:

- Prices or pricing policies

- Marketing strategies

- Production capacities

- Product standards

- Other commercial or sensitive information

10.7.3 Results Achieved Through the Use of Benchmarking

What can a company expect to achieve when using benchmarking? As with BPR, benchmarking emphasizes attaining so-called breakthrough improvements, as shown in Figure 10.37.

Breakthroughs of the type illustrated by the star are usually accomplished by introducing practices that are new to an industry, through generic benchmarking. Some examples are shown in Table 10.4.

Both benchmarking and BPR can induce dramatic changes. Both can lead to radical changes in business processes, and, thus, both constitute a form of reengineering. The main difference is that while using BPR, the contents of the new process are generated internally, whereas in benchmarking, the impetus for the design of the process are collected from external sources. This is illustrated in Figure 10.38. In a sense, you could say that benchmarking gives input to an ensuing reengineering.

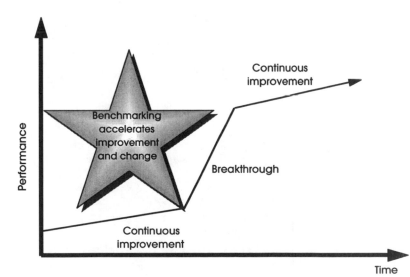

Figure 10.37. Benchmarking versus continuous improvement.

Problem	Compared with
Long admission times in hospitals	Hotel receptions
Lengthy machine setup	Formula One pit crews
Planning the delivery of fresh concrete	Hot pizza delivery
Unstructured maintenance of power turbines	Maintenance of aircraft engines
Difficult to manufacture shell cases with the right cylindrical shape and smooth surface	Manufacturing of lipstick tubes

Table 10.4.   Breakthroughs through benchmarking.

10.7.4 Conducting a Benchmarking Study

Benchmarking is conducted in separate projects whose individual objective is to improve one of the organization's business processes. A benchmarking study includes the activities necessary to:

- Study and understand our own process

- Find benchmarking partners

- Study the benchmarking partners' processes

- Analyze the differences between our own and the benchmarking partners' processes

- Implement improvements based on what was learned from the benchmarking partners

There are a number of models describing the different steps that constitute a benchmarking study. One such model is the so-called benchmarking wheel, as portrayed in Figure 10.39.

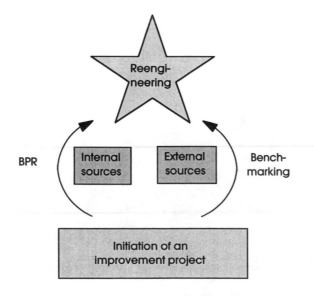

Figure 10.38.   Benchmarking and BPR.

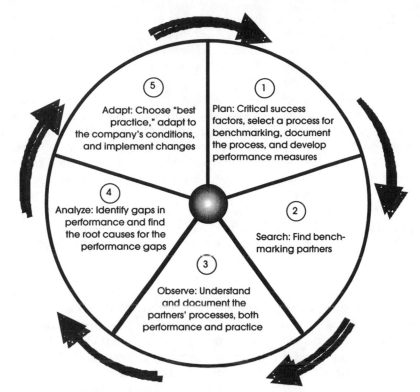

Figure 10.39. The benchmarking process based on the so-called benchmarking wheel.

Ordinarily a benchmarking study lasts between six and eight months, depending on the extent of the process being benchmarked. Often, the implementation of improvements, the main content of the adaptation phase, can take longer. For the other phases, a normal breakdown is that approximately 50 percent of the time is spent on planning, 20 percent on observations of the benchmarking partners, and 30 percent on analysis of collected data. A brief description of each of the phases follows:

Plan

The planning phase contains four basic activities:

1. Select the process to be benchmarked.

2. Establish a benchmarking team.

3. Understand and document the process to be benchmarked.

4. Establish performance measures for the process.

As previously mentioned in chapter 6, benchmarking is one of the tools that gives the most dramatic changes and costs the most in terms of both time and money. Ergo, benchmarking should not be used to improve any business process in the organization, but rather be used consciously for the more critical processes. Step one, by the way, only applies if benchmarking is used as an isolated tool. As this book encourages a more coherent process where improvement needs are identified at an early stage, we can proceed directly to the next step of the planning phase. Thus, no description will be given on how to select a process for benchmarking.

After the process to be benchmarked has been determined, a so-called benchmarking team that will assume the responsibility for carrying out the study must be appointed. The normal size of such a team is between three and eight persons, depending on the scope of the study and the available resources. For composing the team, the guidelines outlined in chapter 2 apply.

The first task for the benchmarking team is to review, understand, and document the selected process, if this has not been done prior to deciding on benchmarking as the tool to use. The final step of the planning phase is to develop performance measures for the process. These will determine the current performance level, compare performance to that of the benchmarking partners, as well as register improvements. Both process documentation and performance measurement have been thoroughly treated already and will not be repeated here.

Based on the tasks included in the planning phase, we can see that like BPR, this general phase must be performed regardless of the improvement tool being used. The benchmarking-specific content appears in the next phase, the search phase.

Search

From the benchmarking wheel, it might seem that the different phases should be performed sequentially. This is not the case. If the entire planning phase is completed before the search for benchmarking partners is started, the progress of the study will usually display a significant drop, as searching for partners usually takes some time. It is recommended that the task of searching for benchmarking partners be started in parallel with the planning, often quite early in the planning phase. The contents of the search phase, are as follows:

1. Compile a list if criteria that an ideal benchmarking partner should satisfy.

2. Search for potential benchmarking partners.

3. Compare the candidates and select one or more partners.

4. Establish contact with the selected partners and gain acceptance for their participation in the study.

The first of these steps is actually a search-technical task. No matter what is being searched for (for example, books in a library or partners for benchmarking) it is preferable to limit the search space. Starting a search among all possible organizations and considering them potential partners can result in an extremely complicated search. It is wise to consider the qualities the ideal benchmarking partner should possess, and consciously search for these. Typical issues that can be included in such criteria are:

- Geographic location

- Size

- Technology used and markets served

- Industry

- Structure and organization

This list could be made endless. However, it is important not to limit the search too much either, as we might exclude partners that could be suitable, if not perfect, for the study.

To find potential partners, a number of sources can be utilized. The organization's own network can usually provide useful information. This pertains to customers, suppliers, and other with which there is cooperation. Different experts within the field can often be of help. Various industry associations possess knowledge about players in the field. Media coverage can give hints, as can all public information. Another hot field in information searching is the Internet. By using carefully selected search keywords, vast amounts of information can be found. In fact, only imagination sets boundaries for the search, although this has its pros and cons. Since the information available is so vast, it is easy to become paralyzed, not knowing quite where to start. Many benchmarking study participants conclude that this phase is indeed difficult and should not be underestimated.

It is also worth considering what performance level we want the benchmarking partners to achieve. The pyramid in Figure 10.40 depicts the number of potential benchmarking partners available within each performance level. For world class, there may be at most only one candidate for each business process, while the number increases rapidly with decreasing ambition level. Thus, it can be much easier to find a moderately good benchmarking partner than holding out for someone of world class ability. A stepwise climb is more reasonable, as it might be close to impossible to go directly to the business processes found among the very best.

Note that there might be many organizations using radically different processes although not achieving any better performance levels. Do not mistake these different processes for better processes and fall into the trap of adopting them.

After having identified a number of potential benchmarking partners, compare and assess them before making a final selection. Often during this phase, a form of performance benchmarking will be carried out to determine how good the different contenders are. Generally, more than one partner is recommended, the usual being between three and five. The costs obviously increase with each additional partner, but they are outweighed by the advantages and the potential for finding the best practice.

The last activity in the search phase is to establish contact with the desired partners for the benchmarking study. There is no sure way to design such a query or to present it to ensure acceptance from the potential partners. An important element is, however, that you are willing to enter into a give-and-take agreement. A willingness

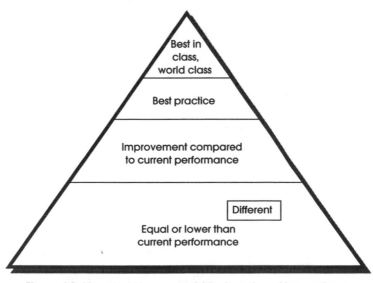

Figure 10.40. Ambition pyramid for benchmarking partners.

to open your organization and share the benchmarking information, increases the likelihood of a positive response.

Observe

This phase is really about documenting the benchmarking partners' process, just as was done for our own process in the planning phase. A little more systematically, the observation phase covers three steps:

1. Assess the information needs and information sources.

2. Select a method and tool for collecting data and information.

3. Perform data collection and debriefing.

In benchmarking, we often say that information is sought at three levels, as shown in Figure 10.41:

- Performance

- Practice

- Enablers

It is important to know the differences between these levels. The performance level is an indicator of how well the organization performs a business process. Drawing a parallel to the world of sports, the performance level can be equated to the finishing time for a sprinter. To learn something and become better, it is necessary to go beyond the performance level and look at how the process is performed, the practice. In the sprinter's case, this equates to the plan for the race, the running technique, type of shoes, and so on. These are elements that can be implemented in our own situation to achieve improvements.

However, there is no guarantee that a process will work in your organization. Therefore, enablers must be captured when studying the process of the benchmarking partners. These are conditions surrounding the process that render the partner able to perform the process in this particular way. Returning to the sprinter metaphor, the enablers can be diet, training methods, and so on that form the basis for the running technique and race plan. If these conditions are not captured, the risk is that lots of

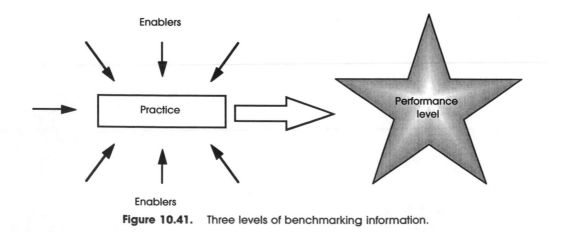

Figure 10.41. Three levels of benchmarking information.

time and money will be spent attempting to implement a new process that cannot work due to lacking enablers.

A number of possible ways are available to collect the information and data about the benchmarking partners. We separate between methods (that is, the means utilized to get in touch with the partner) and tools (that is, which specific technique is used to collect data). The matrix of Figure 10.42 summarizes some of the most common tools and methods, and the X's indicate relevant combinations. Each of these methods and tools is actually a field of its own, and will not be further described in this book.

The last step of the observation phase is debriefing, which happens after data collection from a benchmarking partner has been completed. After having been away from the office for a while because of this task, there are often numerous urgent matters to be dealt with. If these are first attended to, delaying further processing of the collected information, many impressions and ideas can be lost. It is therefore important to set aside time immediately after data collection for a debriefing within the team in order to:

- Collect and sort information and data.

- Transcribe interview notes.

- Take down mental impressions and other ideas not yet captured on paper.

Analyze

After having collected information and data about the benchmarking partners' processes, the next step is to analyze the data material for the purpose of identifying improvement suggestions. The analysis phase actually consists of five steps:

1. Sort the collected information and data.

2. Quality control the collected information and data.

3. Normalize the data.

4. Identify gaps in performance levels.

5. Identify causes for the gaps.

The first two are really preparatory tasks that are included to ensure that all the data is available and accurate. Before starting the actual analysis of the data, it can be pertinent to normalize the data set. A common argument against benchmarking is that

Tools Methods	Questionnaire	Interview	Direct observation
Postal investigation	X		
Telephone	X	X	
Partner visit	X	X	X

Figure 10.42. Methods and tools for the observation phase.

what is being compared is unique, so that no comparison is even close to being relevant. Most things can, however, be compared if a normalization is carried out beforehand. Normalizing means adjusting for the conditions that are truly different. It often consists of recalculating the data to average values or ratios that eliminate aspects like size, market conditions, different legislation, cost levels, and so on.

One central element of the analysis phase is a gap analysis. This entails both identifying gaps as well as determining the causes for these gaps. The gap itself is of little help when it comes to identifying improvement actions. The purpose of the gap is to prove that one partner does something that renders him able to out perform better than another. The presence of a gap is thus more of a signal that there is something worth examining more closely.

There are several techniques available to find the causes for the gap. A relatively simple approach is to compare the flowcharts for the processes directly. This can provide much information about the differences that can contribute higher performance. Other tools that have already been described but that are suitable for this purpose are cause-and-effect charts, relations diagrams, and root cause analysis. Irrespective of the approach employed, the goal of this phase is a list of the conditions believed to contribute to the superior performance levels of the benchmarking partners.

Adapt

As with the planning phase, the last phase of the benchmarking study, the adaptation or implementation phase, is not really benchmarking-specific. Implementation in general is treated in chapter 12, thus, the description here will be very brief. Roughly speaking, the adaptation phase consists of four steps:

1. Describe the ideal process and summarize improvement actions based on it.

2. Set targets for the improvements.

3. Develop an implementation plan, carry out the plan, and monitor the progress.

4. Write a final report from the benchmarking study.

After the benchmarking study has been completed, a final report should be produced that covers the entire study and contain lessons learned and recommendations for future studies. This report will constitute documentation of the study to all parties involved and interested. Furthermore, it should describe further improvement actions that this project did not implement. The document should be sent to the benchmarking partners in return for their participation. Finally, it should contain some record of all benchmarking partners involved and that could become involved in ensuing studies.

Benchmarking is an extremely complex improvement tool compared to some of the simpler chart-based tools presented earlier. There are, however, software packages available to guide benchmarking studies. The author has never actually used any of these in a real-life benchmarking study, but they seem useful. At least two of these have been developed by or in cooperation with experienced benchmarking experts, so they might well be able to convey some useful hints. Software of this type has been designed in connection with both Robert C. Camp and H. James Harrington.

It has from time to time been claimed that benchmarking is a tool mainly applicable to manufacturing companies. This is not correct. Benchmarking

has been used by a number of organization within service industries and government. As an example of a successful application of benchmarking, a description of a study performed by the telecommunications company Pacific Bell in the United States is included.

Pacific Bell is one of several companies offering phone services to the residents of California. It was separated from the AT&T monopoly when the market was deregulated. One means of survival in an increasingly competitive environment has been continuous measurement of customer satisfaction. After using this method since the early 1980s, a benchmarking study was started to look at and improve the system. The basis for the study was a general concern about whether the measurements were accurate and whether they were used sensibly. The benchmarking study is described in the following, phase by phase.

Planning of the Study

First, a benchmarking team was established, consisting of:

- The manager for the measurement department

- Four employees from this department, responsible for areas like collection, analysis, and application of customer satisfaction data

- The central benchmarking manager of the company, who acted as a facilitator of the benchmarking methodology

The first task of the team was to document the current process for measuring customer satisfaction. A very thorough job was done in this respect, resulting in a 17-page description of all processes related to this area. Besides this task, the team members participated in different conferences, seminars, and other events that focused on the topic of customer satisfaction measurement. The result was that the team was knowledgeable about its own processes as well as the field in general by the conclusion of the planning phase.

Search for Benchmarking Partners

To find the best possible benchmarking partners, Pacific Bell defined a list of criteria for the organization and its customer service, constituting a partner profile. For each element on this criteria list, a value was assigned indicating its importance concerning an evaluation of a potential partner. In order of decreasing importance, the criteria related to the company itself were:

- Profitability the last five years, as this was seen as an expression of the degree of customer satisfaction

- Multiple market segments, to find partners operating in a similar situation to Pacific Bell's

- Service industry, as customer satisfaction measurement in the service industries was considered quite different from what was being done in manufacturing organizations

- Long-term customer relationships, as opposed to companies dependent on one-time sales, as long-term relationship would enable a continuous measurement of customer satisfaction

- California-based, as this geographical area has a unique blend of people

- Technology-driven, to resemble Pacific Bell as much as possible

- Changed regulation conditions, to see how such conditions impacted customer satisfaction and the measurement of it

The criteria defined regarding the customer service of potential partners were:

- A leader in customer satisfaction

- Active use of feedback from the customers for process improvement

- A quantitative and systematic system for measuring customer satisfaction

- Using several different instruments for customer satisfaction data collection

To identify potential benchmarking partners, one full-time person was hired to conduct a very thorough search of literature to find companies matching the criteria. This resulted in a list of about 20 companies that seemed to match the profile. These 20 potential partners were divided between the team members to conduct an even more detailed assessment of each. Based on this evaluation, eight organizations were agreed on as objects for further study.

Information Collection

The selected partners belonged to industries like banking, telecommunication, insurance, and public relations. To collect information, a questionnaire was produced consisting of two parts, one quantitative and one qualitative.

The quantitative part focused on figures for the number of employees who performed different tasks, costs, the number of customers followed up, response rates for measurements, and so on. The qualitative part was far more extensive and focused on how customer satisfaction measurement was performed, applied, by whom, specific performance measures used, and so on.

Due to limited means for the benchmarking study, the team found it impossible to undertake the data collection through partner visits. Training was therefore given in interview techniques and the questionnaire was answered by phone and fax. First, the companies agreeing to participate in the study received a document containing Pacific Bell's own answers to all the questions in the questionnaire. Next, the quantitative part was filled in by the partner and faxed back to Pacific Bell. After having examined the answers, the qualitative part was answered over the phone.

Data Analysis

To conduct the analysis in a sensible way—that is, by spending sufficient time on it, early on—a number of full day meetings were agreed to. First of all, the quantitative data were compiled into a matrix and analyzed, which was a rather easy task. The analysis of the qualitative answers was far more complex, where all answers had to be discussed in plenary to create a full understanding of the partners' processes. This phase led up to a list of recommendations regarding issues Pacific Bell should change:

- Establish an organization that could handle all customer responses and use it to improve the products and services.

- Terminate the generation of customer satisfaction data on the level below managers, to avoid the employees' fear for repercussions.

- Stop basing the payment for lower-level managers on customer satisfaction data.

- Develop internal process indicators linked to customer requirements.

- Expand the scope of customer satisfaction measurement, but reduce the measurement frequency to once every three months.

- Survey both customers who had recently been surveyed and those who had not, while also trying to reach the customers who rarely gave any feedback, the so-called "Gold" customers.

- Use customer satisfaction data at a strategic level.

- Eliminate the frustration at lower levels in the organization over being held responsible for measures they could only partially control or impact.

Adaptation and Improvement

Within a month after having presented the recommendations, management agreed to reduce the extent of the questionnaire used for measurement. This led to savings of about $1 million, and thus immediately saved far more than the total costs for the benchmarking study.

More importantly, actions were taken to understand in detail the customers' true requirements for the services delivered by Pacific Bell, as exemplified by the benchmarking partners. Furthermore, pilot implementations were undertaken of a totally new system for customer satisfaction measurement, where the responses were used only at a high organizational level, while the other employees had process level measures developed. A number of less extensive changes were also introduced, regarding measurement of customer satisfaction, related to specific processes for customer service. For instance, a system was established where immediately after installation or repair is completed the customer is notified, a practice that was not common before.

Achieved Results

Based on the highest cost estimate for the study, the costs reached $70,000. The reduction in measurement extent and the introduction of a new measurement system for customer satisfaction are expected to give savings in the area of at least $5 million. Even more important than the savings is the fact that a number of processes were dramatically improved as a consequence of the study, which is expected to result in large gains in terms of increased customer satisfaction. In addition, many of the changes improved the work situation for many employees.

REFERENCES

Akao, Yoji, ed. *Quality Function Deployment: Integrating Customer Requirements Into Product Design.* Productivity Press, Cambridge, Massachusetts, USA, 1990.

American Productivity & Quality Center. *Basics of Benchmarking (Course Material).* APQC, Houston, Texas, USA, 1993.

Andersen, Bjørn, and Per-Gaute Pettersen. *The Benchmarking Handbook: Step-by-Step Instructions.* Chapman & Hall, London, England, 1996.

Aune, Asbjørn. *Kvalitetsstyrte bedrifter* (The title translates to *Quality-Managed Companies*). Ad Notam, Oslo, Norway, 1993.

Griffiths, John. "Driving Out the Old Regime," *Financial Times.* August, 1993: p. 20.

Hammer, Michael, and James Champy. *Re-engineering the Corporation: A Manifesto for Business Revolution.* Harper Business, New York, USA, 1993.

Harrington, H. James. *Business Process Improvement: The Breakthrough Strategy for Total Quality, Productivity, and Competitiveness.* McGraw-Hill, New York, USA, 1991.

Kubeck, Lynn C. *Techniques for Business Process Redesign: Tying it All Together.* John Wiley & Sons, New York, USA, 1995.

Peppard, Joe, and Philip Rowland. *The Essence of Business Process Re-engineering.* Prentice Hall, Hemel Hempstead, England, 1995.

Swanson, Roger C. *The Quality Improvement Handbook: Team Guide to Tools and Techniques.* Kogan Page, London, England, 1995.

CHAPTER 11

Organizational Tools

So far, many different tools, each with varying purposes within the different phases of an improvement project, have been described. Common for all of these are that they have been named, described, or characterized based on the purpose or the content of the tool, and usually centered around a specific procedure or technique. In addition, there are some "tools" where the organization of people in the improvement work is the core approach. The separation between these two types is perhaps not very clear, but in this chapter, these types of tools or approaches will be treated. More specifically, the following are described:

- Cross-functional teams
- Problem-solving teams
- Quality circles
- Concurrent engineering

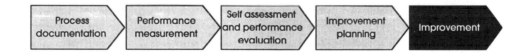

11.1 Cross-functional Teams

An organization must perform a certain set of tasks. The traditional way of structuring the organization "to solve this problem" has been to divide these tasks between different departments. This way, each department has assumed responsibility for a defined portion of the total set of tasks. The department members have been trained and specialized to solve these tasks. This is readily apparent in normal organization charts, where departments like finance, personnel, and procurement can be found.

As soon as people are placed in boxes in an organization chart, it seems as if the lines of the boxes become solid boundaries within which they should stay. Communication across these boundaries is limited and a member of a department will only perform tasks that naturally belong to the parent department's area of responsibility. Each department seeks to maximize its influence and authority, while at the same time the performance level within each department is optimized. The result is often that the sum (the entire organization) is far from the sum of the elements (the departments), and at worst is less. Each department suboptimizes, resulting in conflicting behavior and poor performance for the total organization. At the same time, individual departments are not capable of solving problems involving more than one department.

Before a possible solution to the problem is presented, let us re-examine the two types of variation or deviation discussed in chapter 10. Slightly redefined, we can call these local faults and system faults.

Local faults are deviation that occur as a consequence of a local, identifiable cause. For example, it might take twice the normal time to complete a report, because the person doing it spilled coffee on the almost finished report and had to do it all over again. These are faults beyond the normal variation of the process, and have a clear cause. Some characteristics of such faults follow:

- A control chart will reveal that the variable is out of control.

- There is almost certainly a short-term solution that will work.

- The cause for the fault is often readily identifiable.

- The solution is usually local.

- "Firefighting" can be reasonably successful.

System faults represent the natural variation of the process, faults inherent in the process that must be expected to occur. Solving such problems is not a local task and is rarely easy. Typical traits of system faults follow:

- A control chart will typically show that the variable is under control, but not good.

- A coherent and lasting solution cannot be found locally, management is part of the solution (or perhaps the problem).

- A long-term solution must be found, which often takes a year or more to implement.

- Uncovering the causes for the problem is often very difficult, usually there are several interrelated causes.

- A solution depends on cross-functional efforts.

- "Firefighting" will not help in this case.

System faults are in other words rarely so unidimensional that they can be solved by one person or one department. If the responsibility for correcting system faults is given to someone without overview of the entire situation and involved departments, the result is usually that the responsibility is passed around like a hot potato nobody wants to get stuck with. Furthermore, in mature organizations that have worked with improvement for a while, it is not unusual that the remaining problems are of a cross-functional nature, thus requiring cross-functional improvement efforts. True improvement of system faults often results from efforts in the "white" zones of the organization chart, that is, at the interfaces between departments. The answer to this challenge can often be to form cross-functional teams that possess broader competencies and, importantly, organizational positions.

A cross-functional team can be defined as follows:

A cross-functional team is a group consisting of members from different functional departments or areas of responsibility and often also from different hierarchical levels. The purpose of the team is to solve problems involving several of the organization's functions.

Cross-functional teams can be formed in three different ways or, actually, three different points in time:

1. To exist on a permanent basis, where the entire organization is simply changed to consist of a number of cross-functional teams instead of specialized departments. This is quite rare, but where it has been attempted, the teams have assumed responsibility for both conducting and improving the business processes. Such an organization is thus in accordance with the process organization outlined in chapter 2.

2. On an ad hoc basis, where a team is formed to solve or investigate a specific problem and thereafter is dissolved. This is actually a special variant of the cross-functional teams called problem-solving teams, which is treated in the next subchapter.

3. As a combination of these two, where the team is permanent and its members mainly function within their departments, but from time to time meet within the team. This way, the team will consist for a long period of time and constantly find new cross-functional problems or improvement areas to attack. This last approach is by far the most common one.

The normal and recommended size of such teams is between four and eight people. Permanent teams should be set up to attack a variety of different problems (that is, not assembled to fix one specific problem). There are also some rules governing the work in such cross-functional teams:

- Meetings are held only when there is 100 percent attendance.

- Meetings are held in "sacred" places (that is, not on the home turf of any of the members and somewhere where there are no interruptions).

- Meetings are held during regular working hours.

- Before the team is established, management must agree to follow up on any recommendations made by the team, subject to realistic budgetary constraints.

- Experts can be summoned according to needs.

It must be expected that during the first meeting after the establishment of the team, the work will be theoretical and characterized by the fact that the team and its members are trying to find their places. Such discussions might seem a waste of time but they educate the members and allow them to get to know each other. For each problem attacked by the team, the result should be a list of improvement actions with related cost estimates, a schedule for implementation, and indications of expected results.

11.2 Problem-solving Teams

Cross-functional teams are usually established to find and solve many problems over a long period of time. A problem-solving team, however, is a temporary special variant established to attack a particular problem. In this respect, it can be defined as follows:

A problem-solving team is a temporary team formed to solve a predefined problem and is composed of members from areas affected by this problem.

Both cross-functional teams and problem-solving teams will generally employ many of the tools previously presented to create improvements. The same rules described for cross-functional teams apply to this type of team. The advantages of establishing such a team to handle problems and improvement projects linked to system faults are multiple:

- A specific and collective responsibility for the problem is defined, avoiding turning it into a "hot potato."

- By involving everyone affected by the problem in the team, it is ensured coherent solutions acceptable to everyone are arrived at.

- As the work is carried out in parallel or simultaneously in a cross-functional team, not sequentially in each department, the process is usually relatively quick.

- A positive side effect of this type of task is that the organizational culture and the work climate are usually improved.

11.3 Quality Circles

We defined problem-solving teams as a special variant of cross-functional teams because they are temporary. Similarly, quality circles can be viewed as another special variant, as quality circles are permanent, but not cross-functional. Turning again to definitions, a quality circle can be said to consist of (Aune, 1985):

- A group of people from the same work area (they have the same type of jobs and experience the same problems) who;

- Under the guidance of a circle leader (in the beginning preferably a foreman or the like);

- Voluntarily participate in regular meetings during normal working hours approximately one hour per week;

- To, according to their own priorities, identify, analyze, and solve problems within their own work area and;

- Present oral and written suggestions for solutions with cost estimates to a person authorized to decide on implementation.

The objectives of the work in quality circles are purposefully defined to be twofold:

- Obviously to strengthen the competitiveness of the organization through creating improvements.

- At the same time, to create a good basis for development of the individual employee's creative skills and allow the use of these skills in practical improvement work.

The separation between quality circles and other cross-functional teams is thus quite clear. The cross-functional teams are supposed to attack system faults, often called the "the vital few." Quality circles are supposed to work within their own work area and attack local faults, which are often called "the trivial many."

The normal approach is to establish several quality circles, each having its own circle leader. Above these, there is usually a facilitator that can assist if some of the circles get stuck, who also functions as a point of contact to the management of the organization. Quite often, we can find a steering committee for the circles, which coordinates the entire activity in this area. The committee usually consists of members from management. Putting these different elements together, the organization of the quality circle work will look like Figure 11.1.

It is worth mentioning that a number of organizations in the western world tried quality circles during the 1970s and 1980s, and few still use them. Studies have shown some of the reasons quality circles have not worked well in the West:

- The circles were not part of a larger quality program.

- The circles never became an integrated part of the work in the organization.

- The circles were introduced before the general consciousness level about quality had become sufficiently high.

- The companies were more concerned with the financial gains achievable than the working mode itself.

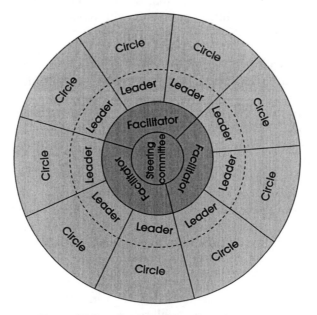

Figure 11.1. Organization of quality circles.

- The work in the circles was perceived to be too bureaucratic and all the imposed rules seemed artificial.

- As the circles succeeded in solving the smaller local problems, they ran out of problems they could attack.

11.4 Concurrent Engineering

Concurrent engineering can be viewed from many different angles and is in itself an entire field. What is interesting in this case is that concurrent also is a variant of cross-functional teams, where the main objective is to improve the result and reduce the time it takes to develop and launch a new product. Thus, the purpose of the tool has already been very clearly defined (that is, it relates to the product development process and the performance level of this process).

If we take a humorous look at how the traditional product development process is carried out, it can be described by the following sequential steps:

- The sales department receives a request from a customer about a new product and passes the request on to:

- The development department, which spends time designing increasingly complex products and passes the specifications across the wall to:

- The planning department that generates plans for procurement and manufacturing.

- The purchasing department negotiates with many suppliers to achieve the lowest prices possible for the necessary components.

- The manufacturing department must use rush orders and overtime to make agreed delivery date, while components with defects from the suppliers must be reworked.

The result is shown in Figure 11.2.

The two most important keywords with regard to concurrent engineering are:

- *Integration*, meaning that the different departments involved in the process from product concept to launch are integrated. Instead of having one department complete its step of the process isolated from everyone else, the departments are integrated into a team that works on the entire process together. This way, the process engineers can impact the product for the highest degree of manufacturability, the sales department can influence the productline with the requirements of the market, and in fact, the customer can be allowed to impact elements like maintenance friendliness, usability, and so on. This way, the integration will mainly contribute to a better quality of the result from the product development process.

- *Parallelism*, which mainly reduces the duration of the process. By performing tasks in parallel instead of sequentially, the duration is automatically reduced. At the same time, the integration will reduce the need for rework and changes,

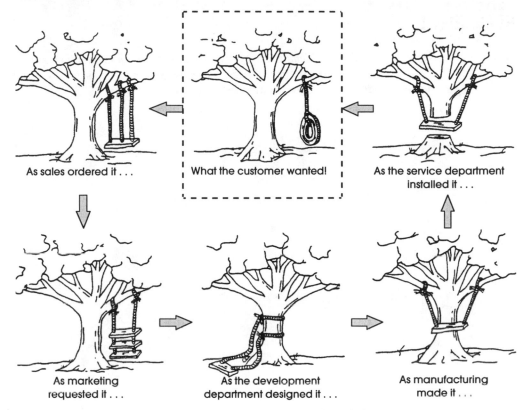

As sales ordered it . . .

What the customer wanted!

As the service department installed it . . .

As marketing requested it . . .

As the development department designed it . . .

As manufacturing made it . . .

Figure 11.2. A possible result from poor communications during product development.

because everyone's views are already represented in the process, thus further reducing the product development time.

A typical integrated team within concurrent engineering will consist of:

- A sales representative
- A market analyst
- Two product developers
- A process engineer
- The manufacturing manager
- One manufacturing operator
- A customer

This team will assume the collective responsibility for performing the product development job. In addition, literature on concurrent engineering describes different specific tools that can be used in this process, but these are beyond the scope of this book.

The purpose of this chapter has mainly been to show that there are tools related to the way work is organized, both in general and during improvement.

REFERENCE

Aune, Asbjørn. *Kvalitetssirkler: Problemløsningsgrupper for personlig vekst, kvalitet og produktivitet* (The title translates to *Quality Circles: Problem Solving Teams for Personal Growth, Quality, and Productivity*). Universitetsforlaget, Oslo, Norway, 1985.

CHAPTER 12

Tools for Implementation

All the previous categories of tools have to some extent been aimed at creating solutions or improvement actions to solve different problems. If these improvements are not implemented in the organization, the entire effort is wasted. Excellent improvement suggestions do no good lying in a drawer or on a shelf, they must be brought to life. This is no doubt a very difficult task, and will actually consist of several subtasks:

- Sorting and prioritizing among the improvement proposals

- Organizing the implementation

- Setting targets for the improvements

- Developing an implementation plan

- Creating acceptance for the required changes and a favorable climate for the implementation

- Carrying out the implementation itself

This chapter will address some general questions related to these tasks and partly describe some specific tools. The tools available for this phase are:

- AΔT analysis

- Tree diagram

- Process decision program

- Force field analysis

The remainder of this chapter contains a blend of descriptions of the more general tasks in the implementation phase and the more common tools. The first decision

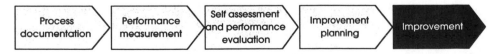

to be made in the implementation phase of an improvement project is usually what to implement. Often, the work of the preceding phases will have generated a number of possible actions. Rarely will the resources required to implement all suggestions be available. It is therefore a natural first step to prioritize the improvement proposals and start with those expected to produce the greatest effects or that for some other reason are preferred. Criteria that can be used for sorting the proposals are:

- The investment needs for introducing a new method or process
- The training needs for a new process
- Time limitations, both in the form of deadlines for the project and organizational restrictions with regard to the time available for performing the implementation task
- The organizationís motivation level (that is, burned out or still enthusiastic)

Such a sorting will give a prioritized list of improvement actions in the order they should be implemented. There are several alternatives available when it comes to deciding how the implementation should be organized:

- By the original improvement team, where the same team that has carried out the project so far also undertakes the implementation of improvements. The advantage of this approach is that the team knows the project and what the solutions entail.
- By a specific implementation team, where a new team is formed consisting of the necessary and suitable persons to assume the responsibility for the implementation itself. Even if this team does not know the work so far, it is often wise to use or at least include other persons for the implementation than during the development of improvement proposals. Thus, this approach can be sensible in some cases.
- In the line organization, where the functionally responsible persons assume responsibility for implementing changes by using the resources of the ordinary organization. This is perhaps the most common model, where we ensure that those who will later perform the process also take part in implementing it.

After having selected the model for organizing the implementation, the next logical step is to set targets for the improvements (that is, which performance level we want to achieve after the implementation has been completed). For this purpose, AΔT analysis is a helpful tool.

12.1 AΔT Analysis

This is a tool that is quite closely related to both idealizing and value-added analysis. However, while both of these tools are used to create improvement proposals, the main purpose of AΔT analysis is to set ambitious targets for the improvement work.

The method is based on the assumption that it is always possible to find two durations, accumulated costs, total number of defects, or other accumulated performance measures for a given process:

- "A" stands for *actual* (that is, the actual time, costs, and so forth, currently related to performing the process to be improved).

- "T" stands for *theoretical* (that is, the theoretically fastest time, lowest cost, and so forth, that can be achieved when performing the process).

Defined this way, we see that the theoretical value is closely related to the ideal process in idealizing. Furthermore, if considering only time or cost, the theoretical value can often be found simply by subtracting OVA and NVA identified through a value-added analysis. The analysis can be used in conjunction with these two tools.

When performing an AΔT analysis, these two values can be used in two different ways. First of all, we can calculate the ratio between the A and the T value:

$$\Delta = \frac{A}{T}$$

This ratio, Δ, expresses the improvement potential in eliminating all unnecessary activities and performing the process as efficiently as possible. The higher the ratio, the higher the potential. This ratio can also be used as an expression of how much there is to gain by approaching the ideal process.

For setting improvement targets, there is no need to calculate Δ. Instead the target can be based on the T value. Whether the target should be set at the T value (or somewhat below to take into account any practical limitation) is an assessment that must be done in each specific situation. The steps of the analysis will be:

1. Start the analysis from the flowchart for the current process.

2. In the flowchart, add figures for time, cost, number of defects, and so on for each activity.

3. Evaluate critically each activity to determine whether it adds value or not. If not, determine whether or not it can be eliminated. Activities that can be eliminated are marked with a marker or by some other suitable means.

4. Summarize the A values and the T values, where the T values are all the non-marked activities, and calculate the ratio A/T.

5. Set the improvement target at or close to the T value.

A company that had reached the implementation phase of an improvement project had some problems determining an improvement target for a reduced process duration. A suitable tool for this task turned out to be the AΔT analysis, as the company both had produced a flowchart for the process and partly performed a value-added analysis. The flowchart with attached activity duration times and activities eligible for elimination marked is shown in Figure 12.1. As can be seen, the ratio between A and T was 2.05, that is, a potential for approximately halving the duration time for the process. To be a little more realistic, the target was reduced somewhat compared to the ideal, down to 12 days.

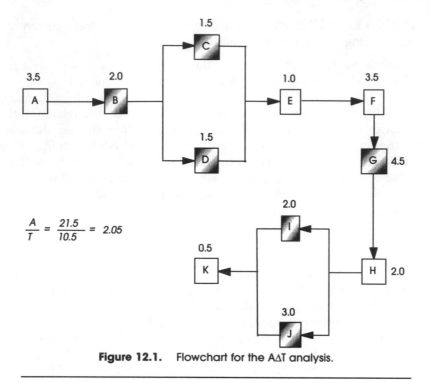

Figure 12.1. Flowchart for the AΔT analysis.

When it comes to improvement targets, or targets in general, they should be:

• Ambitious enough to require some effort to be reached. Targets that are too easily attainable will not pose any challenges and rarely inspire great motivation. The result can therefore be a lower improvement gradient than what could have been the case had the targets been more ambitious.

• Realistic, on the other hand, so as to not deter. Targets that are too ambitious to ever attain can cause the pendulum to swing too far to the other side, leading to frustration and reduced effort.

• Operative, to be easy to comprehend and follow up, to monitor whether we are approaching the target.

It has been claimed that when Ronald Reagan won his first presidential election in the United States, he gave all federal offices instructions to increase productivity 5 percent within one year. After a year had passed, the results starting ticking into the administration office, and most of them were between 4.8 and 5.2 percent productivity increases. The target of 5 percent was probably not sufficiently ambitious, and a target of 10 percent would probably have resulted in figures between 9.8 and 10.2 percent. By setting the target too low, it did not inspire and motivate sufficiently to reap the full effects possible. If, on the other hand, the target had been set at 50 percent, the results might still have been in the vicinity of 5 percent, as it would have been asking too much, creating frustration.

12.2 Tree Diagram

Any project should have a project plan, as has been emphasized already. This is also true for improvement projects, and not in the least the implementation phase of such a project, which can often be viewed as a project of its own. Implementing improvements can often take longer than the total duration of the project thus far. It is therefore essential to have a project plan to guide this activity.

Generally, an implementation plan should be drawn up covering the following elements:

- *Activities*—activities that need to be carried out to implement the improvement proposals generated in the improvement project.
- *Sequence*—the order in which the activities must be carried out.
- *Organization and responsibility*—an indication of who is responsible for each activity, both carrying it out and monitoring the progress.
- *Schedule*—a more detailed plan for when the activities should be carried out, including milestones for central results expected throughout the project.
- *Costs*—estimates for the costs involved in the implementation.

There are several different techniques for project planning, involving different levels of scope and complexity. One easy-to-use tool, suitable for breaking down larger tasks into activities of manageable size, is a tree diagram. This diagram can also be combined with more complicated calculation methods for the project, for example PERT or CPM. The approach for creating a tree diagram is as follows:

1. Generate a list of activities that must be performed to implement the improvement proposals.
2. Write down each activity, in the form of a verb followed by a noun, on self-adhesive notes.
3. Arrange the activities in logical subgroups that must be performed in sequence.
4. Arrange the subgroups to an overall sequence to illustrate the entire plan in the tree diagram.

A typical diagram will then look like the one shown Figure 12.2. Tree diagrams can also be constructed using PC software, for instance PFT for Windows.

As Figure 12.2 shows, the result will typically be a hierarchy of activities. The main activities, read from left to right in the diagram, represent the main tasks of the

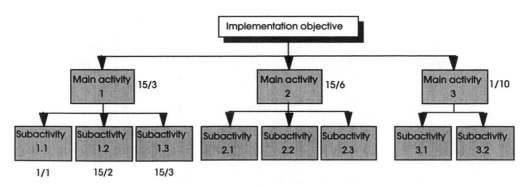

Figure 12.2. A principal tree diagram.

implementation. These main tasks will often be artificial activitie, (that is, names of a group of subactivities). Each of these main activities will therefore include a number of subactivities below them, to be carried out in the order they are presented from left to right. To each activity in the diagram, information about deadlines, responsibility, costs, and so on can be attached.

The library previously mentioned in an example decided to introduce a new computer-based registration system. To plan this task, the employees designed the tree diagram in Figure 12.3. For each activity, the completion date was attached.

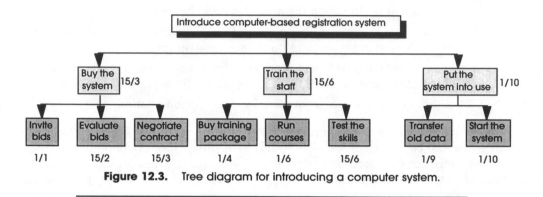

Figure 12.3.   Tree diagram for introducing a computer system.

12.3 Process Decision Program Chart

The plan desired in the preceding example is not very detailed and does not take into consideration any unforeseen events during the implementation. This is actually typical in project plans of this type, that they do not say what to do if something goes wrong. To include this element in the planning, we can use a process decision program chart, often called PDPC. This is a planning tool for making detailed implementation plans that included all possible negative events and problems that could occur along the way. Predicting such problems before they occur makes it possible to address such problems. This enables some form of training in problem solving, which is very inexpensive compared to starting to think about solutions only after the problem has occurred. The PDPC is most often used when a large and complex task is to be carried out for the first time, where the costs associated with failure are exceedingly high, or where finishing by the deadline is critical.

The approach for using PDPC is as follows:

1. Generate a tree diagram for the implementation task or use one that has already been designed. At least to start with, it is wise to use a tree that is not too complicated, as this can require undue time for analyzing possible problems for small, unimportant activities. An appropriate complexity contains the activities with one level below them, as in the example shown in Figure 12.2.

2. For each element at the lowest level of the tree diagram, ask questions like "What potential problems could occur during this activity?" or "What could go wrong here?" For these questions, brainstorm a list of answers for each potential problem area. When no more answers are surfacing, examine the list

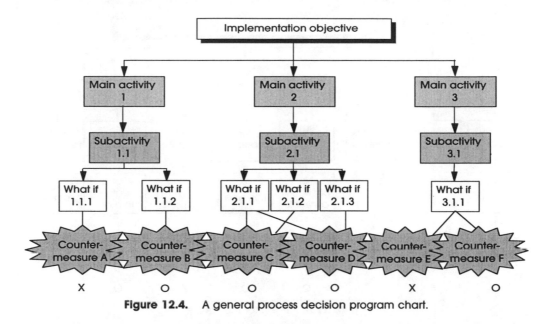

Figure 12.4. A general process decision program chart.

to eliminate problems that it are unlikely or that are expected to have no significant consequences. Each element should include an assessment of the consequences, both in terms of time, cost, and quality.

3. All the remaining potential problems,—those considered significant—to the diagram as "what if"-elements below the lowest level of activities. Use a different to separate these elements from the activities.

4. For each "what if"-element, brainstorm possible countermeasures that can be undertaken if the problem occurs. These countermeasures should consist of reserve activities and indications of duration and cost.

5. Place all countermeasures in the diagram, which is being transformed from a tree diagram to a process decision program chart. Place the countermeasures the "what if"-elements and link them to the potential problems they solve. Again, use a different color to separate them from the "what if"-elements and the activities.

6. Finally, evaluate each countermeasure with regard to ease of implementation, practicality, effectiveness, and so on. Mark difficult ineffective ones with an "X," and mark those you expect to be effective with an "O."

A principal process decision program chart is shown in Figure 12.4. Designing such a chart forces us to anticipate all possible problems that could occur during implementation and, importantly, develop countermeasures. This might change the original plan to avoid potential problems as well as prepare countermeasures in case problems do occur.

The library that designed a tree diagram for introducing a new computer-based registration system, took their study even further and created a process decision program chart for the implementation plan. The chart is shown in Figure 12.5.

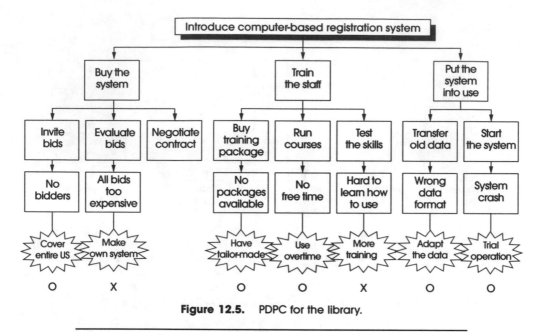

Figure 12.5.   PDPC for the library.

12.4 Force Field Analysis

As mentioned at the beginning of this chapter, an important subtask in the implementation phase is to create acceptance for the suggested changes and a favorable climate for the implementation of these. This is a significant task that involves diciplines such as psychology, human resource management, and so on. This book does not intend to cover such topics, but a general piece of advice is that the more information given to those who will be affected by the changes, the less resistance will be met. Some general advice for creating the desired acceptance of the improvements, is to communicate with everyone affected and anyone that might represent an obstacle to an effective implementation. These are typically:

- Top management, which has the authority to decide on implementation and allotting the necessary resources for it

- Everyone involved in the process to be changed, as it is essential to motivate them for the change

- Everyone delivering input into to the process or receiving output from it, as they could also be affected by the changes

- Other so-called gatekeepers or persons who can impact the implementation and its progress, usually people with financial authority

When it comes to creating a positive climate for the ensuing changes, force field analysis is a helpful tool that can contribute to creating an overview of the situation and possible actions to improve it (Andersen and Pettersen, 1996). Force field analysis is based on the assumption that any situation is a result of forces for and against the current state that are in equilibrium. An increase or decrease in the strength of some of the forces will induce change, a fact that can be used to create positive changes. The procedure for using force field analysis is:

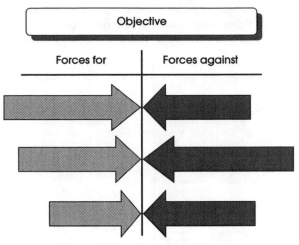

Figure 12.6. Force field diagram.

1. Define clearly the change desired. This is information that can usually be taken directly from the implementation plan and its improvement objectives.

2. Brainstorm all possible forces in the organization that could be expected to work for or against the change.

3. Assess the strength of each of the forces and place it in a force field diagram. The length of each arrow in the diagram expresses the strength of the force it represents.

4. For each force, but especially the stronger ones, consider actions that could increase the forces for the change and reduce those against it.

By implementing these actions, the power balance surrounding the change could smooth the implementation. A principal force field diagram is shown in Figure 12.6.

After identifying potential problems facing the introduction of a new computer system for registering transactions, as well as countermeasures for these, the library finally undertook a force field analysis to understand the climate for this major change. Important forces for the implementation included:

- The new system would dramatically improve the work situation for the employees by simplifying the process of checking books in and out of the library.

- The system would automatically generate reminders for overdue books, thus replacing a currently manual job.

- Searches for titles and other customer services would be quicker and easier.

- If the system worked as anticipated, it would dramatically improve the customer service, which currently had a somewhat tarnished reputation.

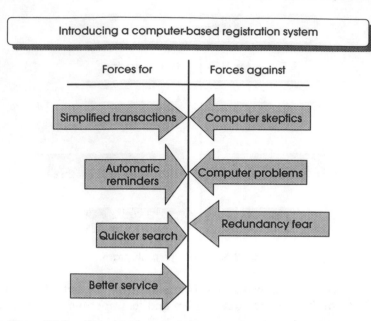

Figure 12.7.   Force field analysis for a new library computer system.

On the other hand, several forces working against it were also identified:

- A general skepticism toward computer tools among many of the employees, whose average age was 42 years.

- Fear of computer problems that could not be solved as easily as with manual systems.

- Fear of becoming redundant due to reduced manpower needs.

Put into a diagram with the forcesí strength represented by the arrow length, the resulting picture of the situation was as depicted in Figure 12.7.

For each of the forces, several measures were identified that could influence them in the right direction (for example, study trips to other libraries where computer systems had already been introduced with good results, general information and training in computer use, and so on).

Finally, some general advice about effective implementation:

- Involve everyone responsible for results from the process that is being improved to ensure full support for the changes.

- Try to elicit involvement and inspiration from those involved in the project.

- Follow a clearly communicated plan.

- Keep the effected persons informed about progress and achieved results.

- Emphasize the importance of patience—changes do not happen over night.

Perhaps the greatest challenge in this phase of the improvement project is to maintain the team's intensity to ensure that the implementation is carried out. Therefore, continuous monitoring of progress is necessary with regard to:

- Time spent compared to the planned duration
- Resources consumed compared to the implementation budget
- The quality of the results

REFERENCE

Andersen, Bjørn, and Pettersen Per-Gaute. *The Benchmarking Handbook: Step-by-Step Instructions*. Chapman & Hall, London, England, 1996.

CHAPTER 13

Using the Toolbox

A paradox about this book is that while it focuses on the many tools available, it is the author's clear view that the tools themselves should not be the focus for improvement work in an organization.

13.1 Isolated Tools Versus a Coherent Process Improvement System

It is inherent to the nature of tools that their purpose is to offer support. To fix a car, select and use the tools that will accomplish the job. The desired result is a car that runs, and it is of no importance whether a wrench, pliers, or screw driver was used. The same way, the desired results for organizations are improved performance and competitiveness. For this purpose, they can use whatever tool fits, as long as it gives results. It is thus far more important to know how to select and use the right tool to reach the set goals than to know about many different tools.

At different events like conferences, seminars, and other fora, claims have been raised that this or that tool is the best, often followed by intense argumentation why. Such statements and allegations are mere symptoms that too much emphasis has been placed on the tool, not its purpose. The fact is that all of the tools presented in this book have different requirements, serve different purposes, are dependent on the situation in which they are applied, and give different results. It is thus not possible to allege that any one tool is the best.

All of these tools belong to a large and well-equipped toolbox available to the organization striving to improve. They should supplement each other and function symbiotically. Which tool is used in a specific situation is dependent on characteristics of the organization using it and the situation in which it is being applied. First, the situation and problem at hand must be defined, then a suitable tool selected for it. If we only have one tool, for instance a hammer, it is amazing how quickly all problems come to look like nails.

The purpose of this book is to present an extensive toolbox for the improvement service man. Coupled with performance measurement and the other elements of the overall improvement model (see chapter 2), this constitutes a coherent process improvement. The challenge is thus to determine which tool should be applied in a given situation. The next subchapter will outline some criteria that could aid the selection task.

13.2 Criteria for Tool Selection

The first and most important criterion is, of course, that the right tool be selected for the purpose intended. It is useful to present the overall improvement model again now that the tools have been discussed. The model is shown in Figure 13.1. As previously explained, this is a cycle that should run continuously in the organization. The explanation of the individual phases differs slightly depending on which phase starts the cycle.

- First, performance planning will be based on input from self assessment, external performance requirements, and other external demands. To obtain this input, the tools of self assessment and benchmarking can be utilized. In the improvement planning itself, there are several tools available, including the performance matrix, spider chart, trend analysis, criteria testing, and QFD.

- Most of the tools presented belong to the phase of performance improvement, and their purpose is to create and implement improvement proposals.

- Performance measurement to follow up the improvements has also been covered.

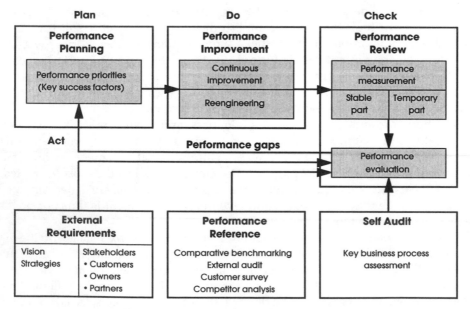

Figure 13.1.   Overall improvement model.

Together this constitutes a complete system for performance improvement where performance gaps are identified, the improvement efforts prioritized, improvements implemented, and the result reviewed, before a new gap is established. The first challenge is therefore to establish this cycle as a natural part of the organization's way of working with improvements. Then the challenge is to select the right tool.

It is also worth repeating that the improvement phase of Figure 13.1 can be divided into several subphases, as shown in Figure 13.2.

Different phases require different tools, thus the central criterion for selecting tools is the tool appropriateness for the situation. Tools for each of the phases are summarized in Table 13.1.

Depending on which phase the project is in and which task we want to accomplish, this table serves as a guideline to what tools are available. When selecting the tool that is best suited to a specific situation, we can look first to the tool itself, asking whether it applies to the given problem. An equally important question is whether the organization possesses the resources necessary to use a given tool. Even if there are no clear answers to these questions, the tools can principally be grouped within the different subphases according to their expected resource requirements, as shown in Table 13.2.

Ideally, one could select a tool based on the characteristics of the organization and the situation in which it will be applied by looking up guidelines explaining which tool is most likely to fit. Unfortunately, the use of and results achieved by all these is not yet clear enough to make such guidelines possible. It is, however, an important area for future research.

In the end, I can only re-emphasize that the tool itself is not important, it is merely a means to achieve improvement. Select a tool that suits the organization and the situation, and then use it. Do not aim to use as many tools as possible or other equally useless ambitions. Finally, the last chapter, chapter 15, of the book contains templates for many of the tools presented.

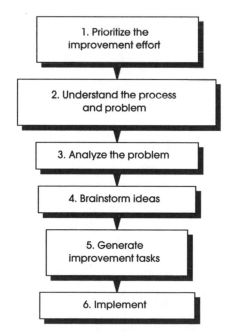

Figure 13.2.   Subphases of the improvement phase.

Prioritizing	Problem under-standing	Problem analysis	Idea generation	Improve-ment proposals	Implemen-tation
Self assessment	Relationship mapping	Cause-and-effect chart	Brainstorming	Streamlining	Tree diagram
Trend analysis	Flowchart	Root cause analysis	Brainwriting	Idealizing	PDPC
Spider chart	Critical incident	Scatter chart	Crawford slip method	QFD	AΔT analysis
Performance matrix	Check sheet	Histogram	Nominal group technique	Work unit analysis	Force field analysis
Criteria testing	Pareto chart	Relations diagram	Affinity chart	Statistical process control	
QFD		Matrix diagram		Business process reengineering	
				Bencmarking	

Table 13.1.   Tools for different phases in the improvement work.

Resource require- ments	Prioritizing	Problem under- standing	Problem analysis	Idea generation	Improve- ment proposals	Imple- mentation
Few resources required	Trend analysis	Critical incident	Cause-and-effect chart	Brainstorming	Idealizing	Tree diagram
	Performance matrix	Check sheet	Root cause analysis	Brainwriting		PDPC
	Spider chart	Pareto chart	Scatter chart	Crawford slip method		AΔT analysis
	Criteria testing		Histogram	Nominal group technique		Force field analysis
			Relations diagram	Affinity chart		
			Matrix diagram			
Average resources required	QFD	Relationship mapping			Streamlining	
		Flowchart			QFD	
					Statistical process control	
					Work unit analysis	
Many resources required	Self assessment				Business process reengi- neering	
					Bench- marking	

Table 13.2.   Resource requirements of different tools.

CHAPTER 14

American University— Improving the Student Satisfaction

Unfortunately it is not easy to find good working examples of the toolbox in a coherent improvement process. As with the literature in this field, there are a number of good case descriptions portraying the use of one or more isolated tools, but very few that illustrate the interplay between the tools. Therefore, this chapter contains a description of an organization, American University, and its systematic use of a coherent system for process improvement. The description based on a real case, but parts of the story are made up. The purpose is to demonstrate the use of different tools in a larger context.

14.1 Description of the Organization

American University is a small university in the United States. It has about 3000 students at the bachelor, master, and PhD levels. The areas covered are social sciences, engineering sciences, and management subjects. American University is divided into six faculties, each containing three to six departments. The university has about 150 professorships, close to 400 other faculty positions, and a technical/administrative staff of about 600 employees.

The body of applicants to American University has been quite stable, although it displayed a small increase the past year. There is, however, an increasing proportion of students who choose shorter studies or who quit or transfer before completing their degrees. American University receives some funding from the state as well as some support from industry and private donations, but the bulk of income comes from tuition fees paid by the students. The university is not among the highest ranked schools in the United States within its areas, but holds a good position above the average.

The immediate challenge was to offensively to increase student satisfaction and to improve the university's ranking, to increase the long-term number of applicants. This chapter describes how American University handled this challenge.

14.2 Improvement Planning

American University had for years based its operations on a form a performance measurement that included:

- National ranking performed by different agencies based on many aspects of the universities

- Development in the body of applicants

- Study completion percentage

- Separate course evaluations

Based on these performance measures, it was difficult to prioritize the areas or processes of desired improvement. At the same time, there was a wish to start carefully with a pilot project, both because of the limited short-term resources for this work and to become familiar with the improvement process. To help prioritize the resources for the pilot project, a better set of performance measures was needed. Ideally, a comprehensive process documentation of important processes should have been undertaken, but the pilot project and the preparations for it did not offer room for this. The university's management team, consisting of core academic and administrative personnel, decided therefore to conduct a measurement of the customer satisfaction of a selection of students. The management team wanted to combine this with input from companies that had hired students graduating from American University over the last two years.

A questionnaire was designed and distributed to about 200 students from different departments. Concurrently, telephone interviews with both alumni and managers from about 20 companies in the area were conducted. Some main areas of evaluation were:

1. Usefulness of the academic content of the studies

2. The faculty's ability to convey the academic message

3. Routines for admissions and other administrative student policies

4. Housing and leisure facilities on campus

5. Pedagogical tools used in teaching

6. Tuition fees and other study costs

7. Relevance of the education for later jobs

8. The students' abilities to cooperate in ensuing work situations

Even though some variation was seen at the start among the faculties, average evaluation scores were calculated for the entire American University. As the competition among universities is fierce, the management wanted to form an impression of the situation compared to other colleges. Many universities collected and published corresponding data in study catalogues and similar material. From such sources, American University collected data from other universities in the state as well as from national competitors. The performance levels were compared with the help of a spider chart, among other, as shown in Figure 14.1.

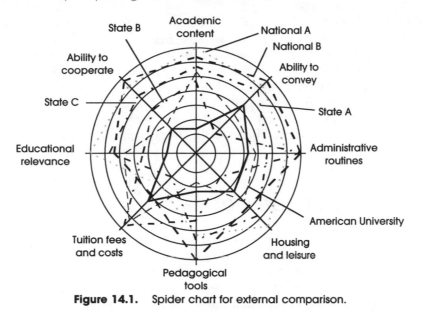

Figure 14.1. Spider chart for external comparison.

In some areas, the results were far from encouraging. The areas displaying the largest gaps were:

- the ability to convey the academic message

- the pedagogical tools

- the administrative routines

- the students' ability to cooperate in later work positions

The results did not indicate what areas should be focused on, so, American University used a performance matrix to prioritize the areas with a gap. The performance matrix is shown in Figure 14.2.

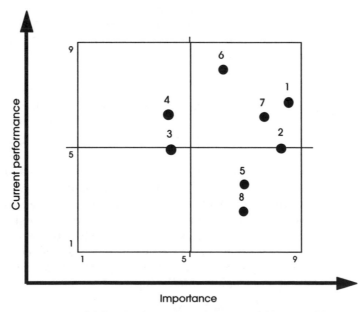

Figure 14.2. Performance matrix for making priorities.

All together, these analyses identified two related areas of abilities for academic communication and pedagogical tools as the areas to focus on. It was assumed that these were somehow connected to the students' lacking ability to cooperate after completed studies. Focus was therefore put on the core process of conducting teaching and knowledge transfer to the students. The Department of Physics was selected as a pilot area. This was a field that could be difficult to teach, and this department had one of the lowest scores at the university and had experienced decreasing applications over the last years. Results developed here would later be applied to the rest of American University.

14.3 Problem Understanding

After selecting the Department of Physics as the pilot area, a work group at the department was established to carry out the project. Together with the central pedagogical coordinator at the university, the work group consisted of:

- Two professors from different academic fields

- One research assistant

- One person responsible for student laboratory work

- Two students at different levels

To enable the group to perform the work, stand-in capacity for the teaching personnel was arranged along with hourly payment for the participating students. Introductory discussions concerning which processes could be defined within the department's teaching activities led to viewing one course from start to finish as a process. As the different courses in the department were organized almost identically, the group decided to start with only one course, assuming that any improvements achieved could be extended to the others.

The first major task was to agree on how the process was currently conducted. As there were, upon closer inspection, some minor differences between courses, the working group chose to document something close to a standard process. Through plenary discussions over a period of three to four weeks, which focused on the level of detail to use, the group arrived at the flowchart shown Figure 14.3, with the following accompanying description:

Before semester start, a brief course planning was performed where lecture topics were defined and other practical details were settled. At semester start, the students taking the course were greeted with an introductory gathering where the course plan and curriculum were presented. The main portion of the time in the course was then spent on weekly cycles of theory lectures followed by a compulsory calculation exercise. The lectures were based on traditional transparency and black board teaching in relatively large classes, often between 100 and 150 students. The calculation exercises were carried out by the individual students on their own and then handed in for evaluation. A number of these were required to be allowed to take the final exam.

Toward the end of the semester, a more summarizing lecture was arranged, where the main content of the curriculum was presented. The courses were concluded with a written exam. This was subsequently graded, and the grade reported to the students. In the case of a failed exam, the exam had to be repeated, up to three times.

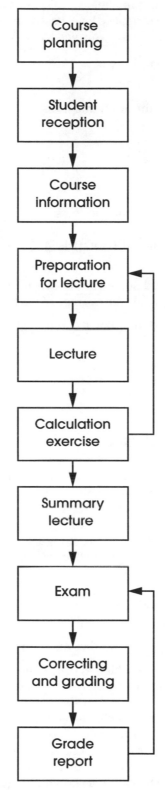

Figure 14.3. Flowchart for the course process.

To enable measuring the improvement project's results, the university management measured the current performance level based on its statistics regarding student grades. On a scale from 1 to 5, where 1 was weak and 5 was strong, the results for the department were as follows:

- Usefulness of academic content: 3.4

- Ability to communicate the academic message: 2.3

- Pedagogical tools: 1.7

- Relevance for later jobs: 3.1

- Ability to cooperate: 1.9

Some central statistical information follows:

- On a grading scale from 1.0 (worst) to 4.0 (best), the average grade at the department was 2.43.

- The average grade varied somewhat between the levels, the average for first year students was 2.28, while the average of the highest-level students was 3.11.

- Within six months after completed studies, 64 percent of the students were employed.

- After completing a Master's degree, 7 percent of the students proceeded to doctoral studies.

14.4 Problem Analysis

To develop an overview of the lacking elements of the pedagogical arrangement with regard to the ability to get the message across to the students, the work group used a fishbone chart. The effect, or problem, causes sought were defined to be a *lacking ability to communicate the academic contents*. Through brainstorming and subsequent discussion and sorting of causes, the diagram in Figure 14.4 was developed.

Each branch will not be further described, but some of the main causes for the problems were:

- The teaching was too theory-focused, with little emphasis on application of theory and industrial use.

- Coherency was missing in the studies and between individual courses.

- Learning was based on old-fashioned principles (for example, one professor per 120 students, pure calculation exercises, and learn-and-forget exams).

To better understand the interplay between the causes and their effects on the problem, a matrix diagram was constructed to analyze the relationships between them. As there were really only two dimensions to the variables, causes and problems, an L-matrix was used, but with the inclusion of a roof matrix to analyze connections between the different causes. The result is shown in Figure 14.5.

The completion of these analyses gave the working group good insight into the underlying causal foundation for the disappointing performance levels. Thus, it

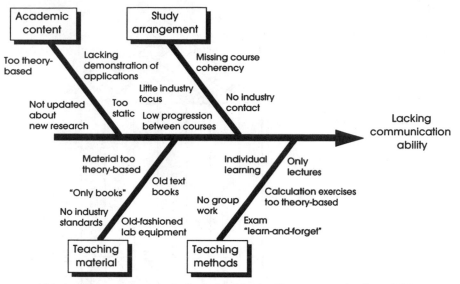

Figure 14.4. Cause-and-effect chart for lacking communication ability.

was concluded that the problem analysis was complete, and the search for solutions was started.

14.5 Idea Generation and Improvement Proposals

The work group envisioned using several improvement tools in this project. From the outset, many group members had ideas about what could be done differently and better, however, few had been clearly formulated and were far from implementation. This potential idea richness led to the assumption that idealizing could be a suitable tool. Using it, the work group could brainstorm the ideal process for academic communication based on the group's latent ideas, then use the results as a basis for improvement.

The idealizing approach was selected and elements of the ideal process were generated through the use of brainwriting. Since the steps of the process was quite independent of each other, ideas could be generated for new ways of doing things at the individual steps. After a two-day written-idea generation gathering with subsequent sorting, grouping, and reformulation of ideas, the group ended up with the following improvement suggestions:

- Starting each course with a three hour motivational gathering where, in cooperation between the lecturer and the students, a common understanding of the course objectives and content would be created.

- Communicating theory through colloquial sessions between the lecturer and a maximum of 15 students.

- Teaching practical applications of theory by solving practical group exercise problems that are presented orally and subsequently discussing solutions.

- Testing with one exam consisting of one individual theory part, oral or written, and one practical group work part with common grading.

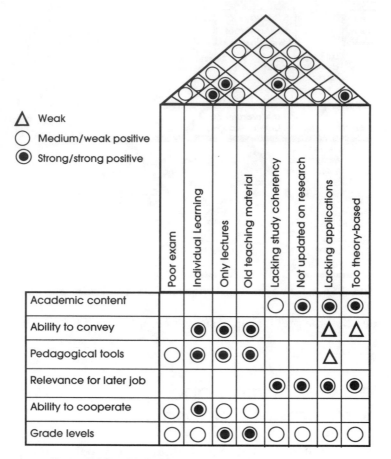

Figure 14.5.   Matrix diagram for American University.

- Encouraging active feedback from the students throughout the course on arrangement and content.

To supplement these proposals with even more suggestions, the work group wanted to perform a process benchmarking of a few other schools. Due to the limited time and money for such an activity, this wish was reduced to a comparison against one other university. The state where American University is located each year presents an award to the higher education institution that has been noticed for exceptional pedagogic merits. This year's award had been given to a small university specializing in industrial management that was located in the neighboring town. A request to this college was favorably answered and American University was welcomed to discuss their ways of teaching. A half day visit with presentations and discussion around a typical course gave the following additional improvement suggestions:

- Within each department, every third year a complete evaluation of the course composition was conducted. During this evaluation, the following issues were focused on:

  - All courses should fit together as a whole.

  - The contents of the individual courses should not overlap too much.

- New research, both at the college itself and elsewhere, should be included in the courses.

- In addition to colloquial teaching, in line with what American University already had discussed, this college also used a system where the students in groups and in turn had to recite the most important aspects of last week's chapter to the rest of the group.

- In courses where this was possible, at the start of the semester, an excursion was arranged to an industrial company or a research institution, where applications of the course's theory were demonstrated.

- Throughout the course, group exercises were based on problems observed during the excursion. At the end of the course, another visit to the company/research institution was arranged where the host organization presented their own solutions to these problems.

- Before the exam, a four hour gathering was arranged for discussion of the curriculum. The exam, however, was organized according to the suggestion from American University about a group exam.

Combining American University's own suggestions, produced through brainwriting/idealizing and benchmarking, created an extensive list of improvement proposals.

14.6 Implementation

The preceding phase, with the resulting set of improvement proposals, was concluded in early October. The objectives for the short-term implementation at the Department of Physics were defined as planning, preparing, and arranging for a new educational system for the spring semester in three of the department's six courses.

The individual lecturers responsible for the courses were appointed the responsibility for this task together with the work group. As these lecturers did not teach any courses in the fall semester, they could devote the next four months to the implementation. To plan the work, a very simple implementation plan was devised that outlined some milestones. Over the next four months, in all three courses, most of the following tasks were undertaken:

- Identifying new and better text books, as well as other multimedia materials.

- Outlining a program for colloquial teaching with smaller classes and student recitation.

- Planning industry and/or research excursions during the semester.

- Producing new group exercises demonstrating practical applications of the theory of the course.

- Preparing the development of a new exam format based on group solving.

- Developing a system for active feedback from the students throughout the semester.

In addition, a gathering was planned for the middle of October, where all the lecturers would debate and coordinate the coherency of the set of courses offered by the department.

Some resistance to the upcoming adjustments was expected from the faculty group, the administration, and the students. In an effort to ease the implementation and the changes it would entail, force field analysis was used. Following a brainstorming of forces for and against, the force field diagram, shown in Figure 14.6 was constructed.

Some countermeasures to these forces were identified as follows:

- New information was distributed to the students about the advantages of the new arrangement.

- Motivational gatherings were organized for the lecturers, where a pedagogical expert would describe experiences from other teaching institutions.

- The rules were changed to facilitate common grading.

Prior to the course commencement in February, practically all of these changes were implemented. The only thing missing was all the preparation necessary for a common exam. There was, however, plenty of time to do this over the course of the semester.

Both after the courses in the spring semester had been completed and in the months following, new measurements of the performance level were conducted. The average results for the three courses were as follows:

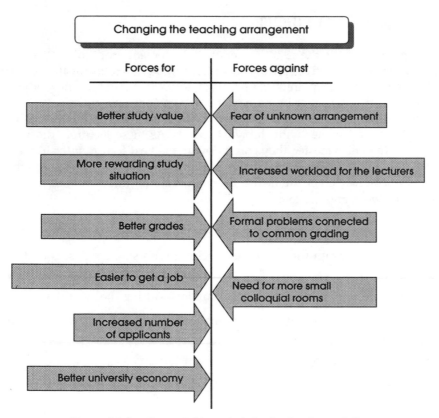

Figure 14.6.   Force field analysis for the implementation.

- Academic content usefulness: 3.9

- Communication ability: 4.5

- Pedagogical tools: 4.4

- Relevance for later jobs (few measures): 4.2

- Cooperation ability (few measures): 3.8

- Average grades: 3.28

As a consequence of this unconditional success, the department management decided to do the same in all the other courses. Simultaneously, the university management wanted the work group to make preparations for and support the same changes at all the other departments at American University. This phase will not be described here.

CHAPTER 15

Template Package

This last chapter contains different templates or forms for tools that can be used in an improvement process. They can either be copied directly from the book, preferably in an enlarged format, or simply function as input for the creation of templates for the individual organization. No explanations on the use of the templates are given in this chapter, as such can be found in the chapter where the specific tool was described earlier on.

Relationship Mapping

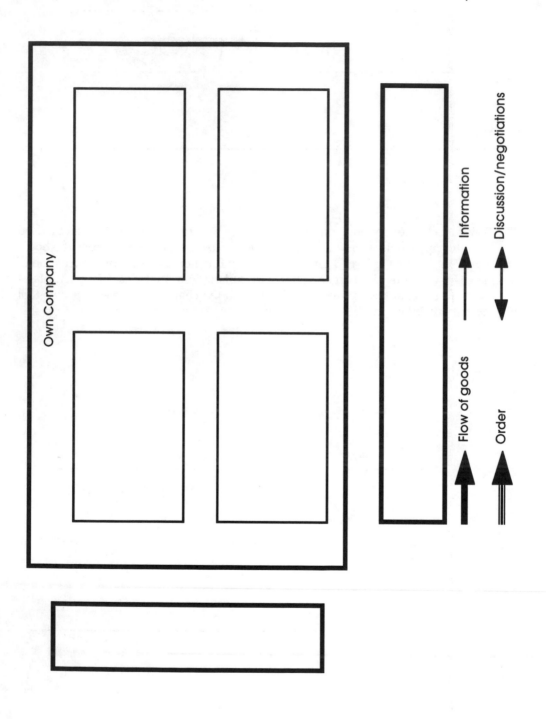

Cross-functional Flowchart

Trend Analysis

Today

Time

Performance

Spider Chart

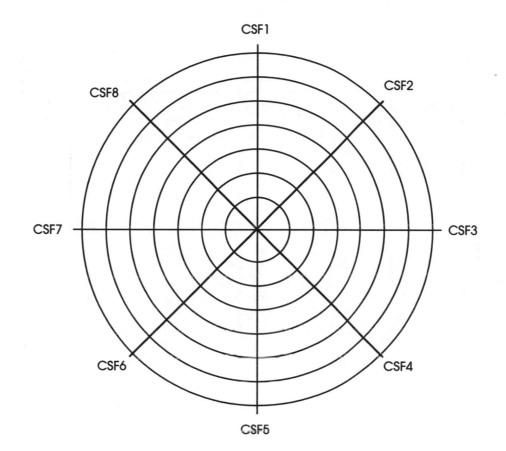

Performance Matrix

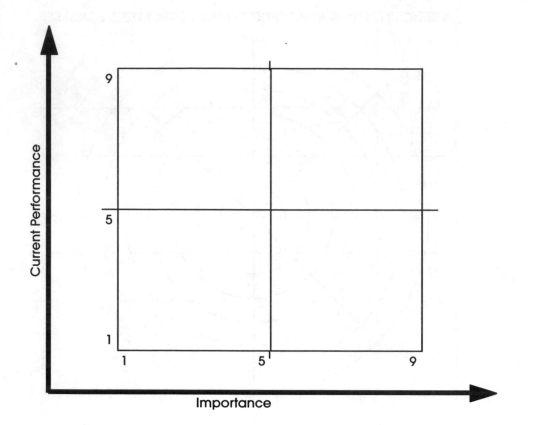

Criteria Testing

Processes	CSF Weight	1	2	3	4	5	Total score
Process 1							
Process 2							
Process 3							
. . . . . .							
Process n							

Quality Function Deployment

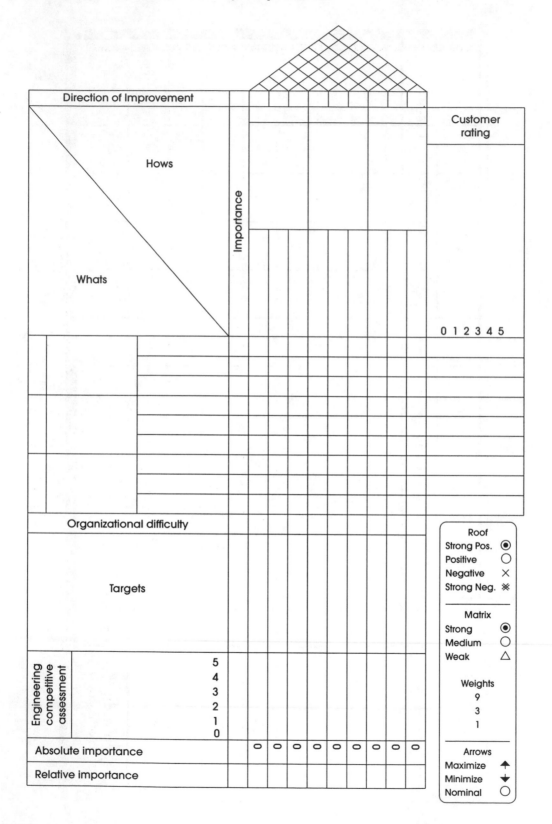

Check Sheet

Problem	Week 1	Week 2	Week 3	Total number of occurrences per problem
Total number of problems per week				

Pareto Chart

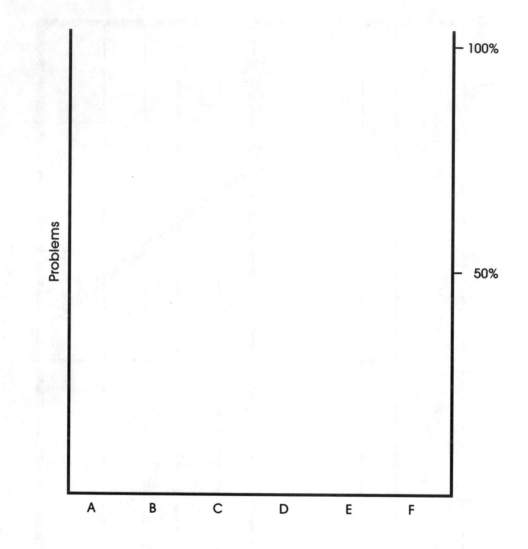

Cause-and-Effect Chart

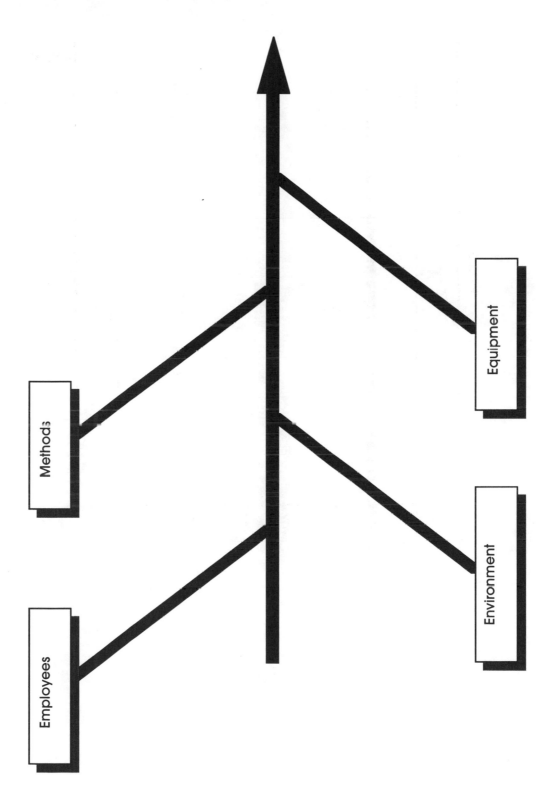

Root Cause Analysis

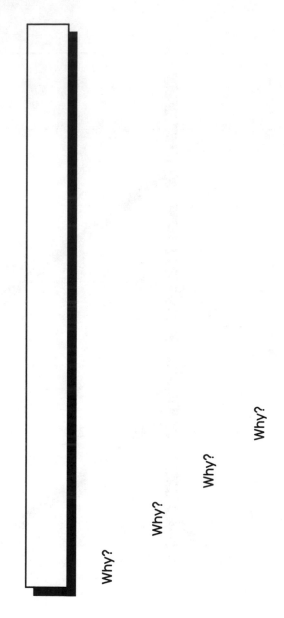

Scatter Chart

Histogram

Category

Frequency

Quantitative Relations Diagram

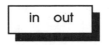

Control Chart

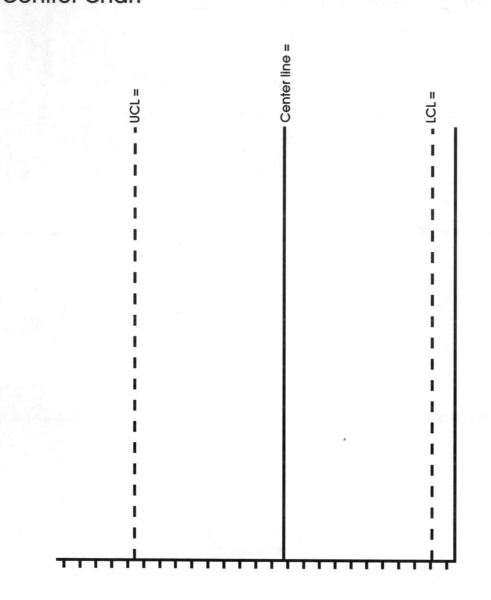

Force Field Analysis

Forces for	Forces against

APPENDIX A

ENAPS Performance Indicators

In this appendix, the performance indicators defined in the ENAPS project are listed. As the intention is merely to give the reader an impression of what performance indicators *can* be used for different business processes, no explanations are provided. For a more thorough presentation of these, consult ENAPS (1997).

#	Indicator	Unit	Formula
	Product Development		
1	Product development lead time	Weeks	N/A
2	Product development effort		(Total product engineering and design cost + total product research cost + total product-related process engineering cost)/Sales
3	Product development reliability	%	Total number of customer complaint-related design changes/Total number of new products
4	Guarantee costs of new products		Guarantee costs of new products/Sales of new products
5	Extent of coengineering	%	Number of coengineered products/Total number of new products developed
6	Patenting performance	%	Number of patents awarded last year/Total number of patents held
7	Contribution of new products	%	Sales of New Products/Sales
8	New product introduction performance	%	Number of unsuccessful new products/Total number of new products
9	Proportion of new products	%	Number of new products developed last year/Total number of active products
10	Number of people in product development	%	Number of people involved in product development/Total work force
11	Product launch target adherence	%	Number of products launched late in the last three years/Total number of new products launched in the last three years

227

| 12 | Components recycled | % | Number of produced components recycled last year/Total number of components produced last year |
| 13 | Multiple usage | % | Number of components with multiple usage/Total number of components |

Obtaining Customer Commitment

1	Customer base growth	%	Number of new customers/Total number of customers
2	Customer dependency	%	The percentage of customers accounting for 80 percent of sales volume last year
3	New customer return	%	Sales to new customers/Sales
4	Lost customers	%	Number of lost customers/Total customers
5	Market share for main product		
6	Marketing cost ratio	%	The marketing cost/Sales
7	Tender efficiency	%	Total tenders value/Sales
8	Tender return	%	Total cost of preparing tenders/Total sales resulting from tenders
9	Tendering hit ratio	%	Number of successful tenders/Total number of tenders
10	Green product sales ratio	%	Sales of products receiving country's green label/Sales
11	Value added per marketing employee	%	(Sales–Purchased material)/Number of marketing employees
12	Customer visits	%	Number of customer visits/Number of customers

Customer Service

1	Product takeback ratio	%	Number of product units taken back/Number of product units sold
2	Product takeback cost	%	Total product takeback cost/Sales
3	After-sales service profit	%	Income from after-sales service/Sales
4	Average complaint response time	Days	
5	Average complaint resolution time	Days	

Order Fulfillment

1	Outgoing delivery quality	%	Number of customer deliveries containing defective parts/Total number of customer orders
2	Outgoing delivery completeness	%	Number of complete customer orders/Total number of customer orders delivered
3	Outgoing delivery timeliness	%	Number of customer orders delivered on time/Total number of customer orders
4	Incoming delivery quality	%	Number of incoming deliveries containing defective parts/total number of incoming deliveries

5	Incoming delivery completeness	%	Number of complete incoming deliveries/ Total number of incoming deliveries
6	Incoming delivery timeliness	%	Number of incoming deliveries received on time/Total number of incoming deliveries
7	Commercial lead time ratio	%	Commercial lead time/Order fulfillment lead time
8	Material procurement lead time ratio	%	Material procurement lead time/Order fulfillment lead time
9	Production and assembly lead time ratio	%	Production and assembly lead time/Order fulfillment lead time
10	Distribution lead time ratio	%	Distribution lead time/Order fulfillment lead time
11	Commercial cost ratio	%	Commercial costs/Sales
12	Inventory cost ratio	%	Inventory costs/Sales
13	Distribution cost ratio	%	Distribution cost/Sales
14	Materials cost ratio	%	Material costs/Sales
15	Production cost ratio	%	Production cost/Sales
16	Supplier payment timelines	%	Number of on-time payments to suppliers/ Total number of purchase orders
17	Customer payment timeliness	%	Number of on-time customer payments/ Total number of invoices
18	Average order value	ECU	Sales/Total number of customer orders
19	Work in progress	%	Cost of Work in Progress/(Purchased material cost + Total production cost)
20	Production efficiency	%	Sum of standard times for all products/Sum of production and assembly lead times for all products
21	Value of canceled orders	%	Value of canceled orders/Sales
22	Percentage rework	%	Rework hours/total production hours
23	Percentage scrap	%	Cost of scrap material/Purchased material cost
24	Energy cost	%	Cost of energy/Sales
25	Production process environmental-friendliness	%	Volume of environmentally-unfriendly material produced/Total volume material produced
26	CO_2 volume	M^3/ECU	Number of cubic meters of oil * CO_2 ratio/Sales

Support Processes

1	System availability	%	Number of hours the main computer system was available/8760
2	Health and safety	%	Number of injuries/Average number of employees
3	Preventative maintenance cost	%	Cost of preventative maintenance/Sales
4	Employee absenteeism	%	Number of man days lost due to absenteeism/ Maximum man days available
5	Employee turnover	%	Number of employees that left the enterprise/ Average number of employees
6	Overtime cost	%	Cost of overtime/Total wages

7	Employee participation	%	Number of employee suggestions/Average number of employees
8	Machine downtime	%	Sum of all machine hours of downtime/Maximum number of machine hours
9	Training investment	%	Training and educational cost/Sales
Evolution Processes			
1	Employee improvement efforts	%	Number employees involved in an improvement project team/Average number of employees
2	Total man-hours spent at management team meetings		
3	Total management team man-hours spent on strategy		
4	Certified suppliers	%	Number of ISO9000-certified suppliers/Number of suppliers
5	Improvement effort	%	Cost of all improvement projects/Sales
6	Suppliers contact	%	Number of suppliers visited/Number of suppliers

Index